The Colors of Life

T0248463

The Colors of Life engages the strategies of Social and Emotional Learning (SEL) to explore life experience through emotion and color. For high-potential readers at the middle school level, the book's humanistic and emotional themes provide valuable complements to the education of STEM-oriented learners.

The book presents color as a vehicle of knowledge and empowerment to foster mindfulness, wisdom, and creative expression in young people. Featuring more than 50 original illustrations, the book's core concepts are reinforced through complementary expressions of language and imagery.

With an accompanying Guide for Teachers and Parents, the book can be accessed individually by independent readers, or it can be used as a teacher-led initiative with creative exercises to be implemented in the classroom.

Marcia Brennan, Ph.D. is a career educator and an award-winning teacher and author. She is the Carolyn and Fred McManis Professor of Humanities at Rice University and the author of ten scholarly monographs and exhibition catalogues. Since 2009, she has served as Artist In Residence in the Department of Palliative Care and Rehabilitation Medicine at the M.D. Anderson Cancer Center.

The Colors of Life

Exploring Life Experience Through Color and Emotion

Marcia Brennan, Ph.D.

Illustrations by Hannah Li and Madison Zhao

Routledge
Taylor & Francis Group

NEW YORK AND LONDON

First published 2025
by Routledge
605 Third Avenue, New York, NY 10158

and by Routledge
4 Park Square, Milton Park, Abingdon, Oxon, OX14 4RN

Routledge is an imprint of the Taylor & Francis Group, an informa business

ISBN: 978-1-032-60924-9 (pbk)
ISBN: 978-1-032-61369-7 (ebk)

DOI: 10.4324/9781032613697

Typeset in Times New Roman
by Deanta Global Publishing Services, Chennai, India

For Amanda Hohlstein
And for all who work to help keep magic in the world for children and adults

Contents

Acknowledgements   ix

Invitation to the Schools of Color: Some Things You Might Want to
Know About Why I Wrote This Book For You   1

1 The School of Red: Passion, Strength, Vitality, Responsibility, and
Resilience   6

2 The School of Orange: Creativity, Empathy, Sensitivity, Emotional
Expression, and Communication   16

3 The School of Yellow: Self-Respect, Autonomy, Ethics, Innocence,
and Vulnerability   25

4 The School of Green: Attunement to Living Systems and the Natural
World   33

5 The School of Blue: Exploring Your Depths, Extending Your Heights,
Expanding Your Power   42

6 The School of Indigo: Shadows, Doublings, Dreams, Fairy Tales, and
the Subconscious   49

7 The School of Violet: Growth and Change, Transformation and
Manifestation   58

8 The School of Silver: The Visionary Qualities of Alchemy and
Reflection   67

9 The School of Gold: Reimagining Values, Treasures, and Transitions   75

10 The School of Pink: Compassion, Care, Generosity, and
the Superpower of a Loving Heart   82

11 The School of Black and White: Bending Light, Flicking the Switch,
and Seeing Multiple Perspectives at Once   89

12 Putting the Pieces Together to Build a House Made Out of Color   95

Contents

(There Is No) Conclusion: The Magic of Your Favorite Colors:
Chromatics, Gratitude, Illumination   99

P.S. Guess What I Just Told Your Teacher?   105

Note Regarding Issues of Confidentiality   109
About the Author and Illustrators   110
Description of *The Colors of Life: Exploring Life Experience Through Color and Emotion*   112

Acknowledgements

The story of this book begins with two of my former students bringing very different matters to my attention. Elisabeth Papadopoulos is a brilliant writer and multidisciplinary creator who generously invited me to serve as a Story Consultant for an animation project she was developing with a major Hollywood studio. Shortly afterwards, Tiffany Padilla made me aware of some of the considerable challenges faced by young people today who have literally grown up with cell phones in their hands. By opening up a difficult conversation, Tiffany opened my eyes to a very important part of life itself. My deepest gratitude goes to Elisabeth and Tiffany for getting this party started!

Throughout the writing process, I have worked extensively with Amanda Hohlstein as a conversation partner, guide, and counselor. I have learned so much from Amanda's brilliant and generous presence, and these books are dedicated to her.

Shortly after the writing process began, I searched for an illustrator to bring the visual aspects of the project to life. While I was hoping to find one gifted visual artist to work with, I ended up finding two. I could not be more thrilled or grateful to have Hannah Li and Madison Zhao as creative partners. Their images are not only remarkable in and of themselves, but their unique stylistic approaches complement one another in intriguing ways that add visionary dimensions to the project.

The content of this book has been shaped in meaningful and important ways by my editor, Rebecca Collazo. She has my deepest thanks for her guidance and support. At Routledge, I am also grateful for the support that this project received from Sophie Ganesh and Alex Andrews. Quinn Cowen has been a skillful and wonderful presence throughout. My gratitude also goes to Sathish Kumar, Manibalan Saqadhevan, and Bryan Moloney for expertly guiding this book through the editorial and production processes. In addition, I would like to thank the four anonymous readers who provided valuable suggestions during the peer review process.

I am extremely grateful for the support of my institution, Rice University. Elaine Palinkas Sanches and Nicole Switzer handled various administrative matters with great care and skill. Diana Heard offered her unfailing warmth and encouragement from the very first moment she heard about the project. Amanda Focke of the Woodson Research Center has been a wonderful supporter and conversation partner, and Dara Flinn and Sylvia Podwika were instrumental in producing high-quality scans of the images. They all have my sincere thanks, as does Cory Eckert, who generously shared her perspective as an author and children's librarian.

My family and friends have also been wonderful. My love and gratitude go to my sister Camille Gagliardi, and to my cousins Alison Healey and Elisabeth Zimmer. I am also grateful to my friends, students, and colleagues Martha Aschenbrenner, Jose Chapa, Karen Cottingham, April DeConick, Neil Holt, Anne Klein, Grace Li, Pat McKenna, Kimberly Mendoza, Brian Ogren, Marcie O'Malley, Kirsten Ostherr, Bill Parsons, N.J. Pierce, David Qin, Rishab Ramapriyan, Ariah Richards, and Jennifer Wheler—and I am especially grateful for the excellent feedback provided by their children Gavin O'Malley and Charlotte Wheler. These young people have kindly served as literary consultants for the project.

My husband, Scott Brennan, has been an ongoing source of love and support. Over the years I have written so many books and I have said this so many times, but Scott, thank you with all my heart, once again, and for always.

Invitation to the Schools of Color

Some Things You Might Want to Know About Why I Wrote This Book For You

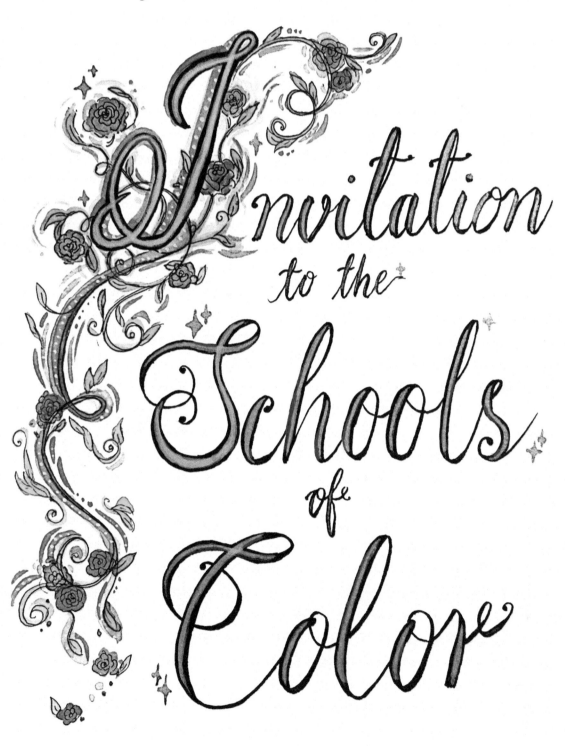

DOI: 10.4324/9781032613697-1

What if I told you that you could explore the color blue for a thousand years?

Red for a thousand years?

Yellow for a thousand years?

What if I told you that there were many different levels of learning, and that you could go through elementary school level, middle school level, high school level, or even college level in the different schools of color? Would you want to know more? If the answer is yes, then I have some wonderful news: You have just been invited to enter the Schools of Color!

Color can be an amazing gateway to life experience. Perhaps when you look at the world, you see the depths in things? Perhaps you also *feel* the depths in things? Perhaps when you look closely you see that the world is a wonderful place, full of fun and incredible creations?

Sometimes in life, it can feel like beams of light hit our field and they turn into color and emotion. Everyone can relate to this experience. Such moments can be powerful bridges between the outer and the inner worlds—between the solid material world that we see with our eyes and experience with our senses, and the invisible inner realms of thought and feeling that each person experiences uniquely for themselves.

Just as color and emotion are both ordinary and extraordinary, concrete and abstract, these subjects are also extremely relevant and practical. I am a teacher, and in part, I wrote *The Colors of Life* to help inspire you, the next generation of students, both personally and in the jobs that you will hold one day and the skills you will need. There is literally nowhere you can't take the subjects of color and emotion. This is the case whether you pursue a career in medicine, education, law, psychology, business, sports, science, engineering, publishing, media, or the arts.

Let's say, for example, that you are considering a career in healthcare. Both the Association of American Medical Colleges and the Accreditation Council for Graduate Medical Education (the latter being the body responsible for the training of resident-physicians) have identified a set of core competencies within pre-medical and medical education.[1] These themes resonate strongly with the subjects of this book as they relate to key issues concerning responsibility and service, resilience and perseverance (red); sensitivity, emotional acuity, and the related capacity for listening and communication (orange); vulnerability, respect, and ethical concerns (yellow); attunement to living systems and the natural world (green); intelligence and critical thinking abilities (blue and indigo); the capacity for growth and change (violet and silver); understanding the significance of compassion and care (pink); and the ability to see multiple, diverse, and sometimes competing perspectives at once (black and white).[2] As you can see, color and emotion can be extremely powerful vehicles of knowledge, wisdom, and creative expression. This book teaches you how to extend these themes into life and into meaning, and how to believe them soulfully.

To approach these subjects in a clear and accessible manner, the structure of this book is prismatic. In addition to the seven primary spectral colors, *The Colors of Life* examines pink, silver, gold, and black and white. Throughout the book, I tell many stories that are drawn from my own life experiences. I also share stories that other people have told me; other people's words appear in italics, as non-rhyming poems. As you read the stories, I want you to think about how these themes appear in your own life. Color and emotion are everywhere, all around us. Your life is filled with these subjects just as much as mine is, or anyone's.

In each chapter, discussions of the individual colors are followed by accompanying exercises featuring Experiential Learning Activities, Visualizations, and Reflections. These sections provide opportunities to explore powerful emotions such as confidence, anger, self-respect, vulnerability, strength, compassion, generosity, wonder, gratitude, humility, and many others. To make the most of this experience, you should plan to keep a journal to record your responses, and to note any significant shifts in your thinking and the insights that emerge. You may just surprise yourself. As you work through the book, please do not feel like you have to answer all of the questions or complete all of the activities in any given section. Just focus on the ones that appeal to you, or that you feel particularly drawn to. Please also remember that journals are private spaces that can be shared selectively. Your writings are pieces of yourself, and your words can be seen as direct extensions of your own mind and heart. Treat them with great kindness and care.

Please come in now. The School of Red awaits us, and we will look more closely at the power of a beating heart.

Notes

 1 In certain places in this book, I include a Fancy Pants Reference Point to provide additional information and to document sources of knowledge. On these subjects, see the American Association of Medical Colleges' statement on "The Core Competencies for Entering Medical Students" at: https://www.aamc.org/services/admissions-lifecycle /competencies-entering-medical-students; Michael S. Kavic, MD, "Competency and the Six Core Competencies," *Journal of The Society of Laparoscopic & Robotic Surgeons* 6 (no. 2, April–June 2002), pp. 95–97: https://www.ncbi.nlm.nih.gov/pmc/articles/PMC3043418/; and *Health Professions Education: A Bridge to Quality*, eds. Ann C. Greiner and Elisa Knebel (Washington, D.C.: National Academies Press, 2003), ch. 3: https://www.ncbi.nlm.nih.gov/books/NBK221528/. I am grateful to Ariah Richards for bringing these resonances to my attention.

 2 Fancy Pants Reference Point: Building on these themes, the Association of American Medical Colleges has endorsed the incorporation of humanistic knowledge into the theory and practice of medicine and medical education. In a report on *The Fundamental Role of the Arts and Humanities in Medical Education*, the authors observe: "Now more than ever, physicians must learn to interweave their developing

scientific knowledge with emotional intelligence, critical thinking skills, and an understanding of social context. The integration of the arts and humanities into medicine and medical education may be essential to educating a physician workforce that can effectively contribute to optimal health care outcomes for patients and communities". See Lisa Howley, Elizabeth Gaufberg, and Brandy King, *The Fundamental Role of the Arts and Humanities in Medical Education* (Washington, D.C.: Association of American Medical Colleges, 2020), p. 1. For a suggestive discussion of the ways in which medical students' exposure to the humanities correlates with positive personal qualities—such as wisdom, empathy, enhanced emotional and spatial skills, and tolerance of ambiguity—see Salvatore Mangione et al., "Medical Students' Exposure to the Humanities Correlates with Positive Personal Qualities and Reduced Burnout: A Multi-Institutional U.S. Survey," *Journal of General Internal Medicine* 33 (vol. 5, January 2018), pp. 628–634.

Reference list

American Association of Medical Colleges. "The Core Competencies for Entering Medical Students." (2022). https://www.aamc.org/services/admissions-lifecycle/competencies-entering-medical-students.

Greiner, Ann C., and Elisa Knebel. *Health Professions Education: A Bridge to Quality*. Washington, D.C.: National Academies Press, 2003.

Howley, Lisa, Elizabeth Gaufberg, and Brandy King. *The Fundamental Role of the Arts and Humanities in Medical Education*. Washington, D.C.: Association of American Medical Colleges, 2020.

Kavic, Michael S. "Competency and the Six Core Competencies." *Journal of The Society of Laparoscopic & Robotic Surgeons* 6, no. 2 (April–June 2002): 95–97. https://www.ncbi.nlm.nih.gov/pmc/articles/PMC3043418/.

Mangione, Salvatore, et al. "Medical Students' Exposure to the Humanities Correlates with Positive Personal Qualities and Reduced Burnout: A Multi-Institutional U.S. Survey." *Journal of General Internal Medicine* 33 (vol. 5, January 2018): 628–634.

Chapter 1: The School of Red

Passion, Strength, Vitality, Responsibility, and Resilience

In this world, we marvel at rainbows. Rainbows are places where light takes form, as color. If you were to look at the far edges of the tonal spectrum—at the outer band of a rainbow—you would see the color red. Red is the color of vitality. It is strength. It can also be power. Sometimes we think of red as an imperial color. Kings and queens of old wore red robes and everyone knew how powerful they were. Red is the color of fire and blood. Blood is the fluid that holds all of the vital nutrients of the body. Sometimes when we are seeing red, it is the color of passionate anger. Red is the color of passion and vitality.

In nature, we don't often see a lot of red. Perhaps this is why we get excited when we see a ripe strawberry, cherry, or raspberry, or a bright red beet, or the vibrant center of a Swiss chard. Red fruits and vegetables are so beautiful, but in nature we only see a splash of red here and a splash there, like a cardinal flying through the green.

One day I met an elderly man who told me a very moving story about why he loved cherry pie so much. For this man,

DOI: 10.4324/9781032613697-2

Everything Comes Alive With Cherry Pie

My image is of a big piece of homemade cherry pie,
About four inches high and three inches wide,
With a nice homemade crust on it.
The crust is a nice, crispy, crystally-looking brown,
Because of the baked sugar.

My mom was a great cook,
And she made some of the best cherry pie I've ever tasted.
Hopefully, no one got to the pie while it was cooling on the windowsill.
The pie was filled with bright red cherries that looked delicious.
The cherries were sweet and juicy and a little bit tart.

When you eat cherry pie,
The cherries pique a burst of flavor,
And then, everything comes alive.

This brings me wonderful memories of home.
The cherry pie is heartwarming.
It's satisfying.
It's tasteful.
And, it's all a gift.

For this man, a whole world of meaning and feeling was contained within a slice of cherry pie. This cherished image grounded the man in sweet, deeply rooted memories of home and family. The pie brought him a heartwarming sense of comfort, and it connected him to a powerful life force that was so strong and vibrant that everything "came alive" when he tasted the pie. In turn, this story gives you a sense of how the vital subjects of love and life can be experienced both in memory and through the senses—in this case, through sight, smell, and taste. This story also shows you some of the magic of the color red, and it gives you a hint of the energies of the color orange, which you'll read about in the next chapter.

Red is the color of the vitality of life. Like a baked cherry pie cooling on the windowsill, red is often associated with the *inside* of things, rather than with the *outside* of things. Even our blood is inside our body. We are *very* red inside our bodies, although we don't usually see it.

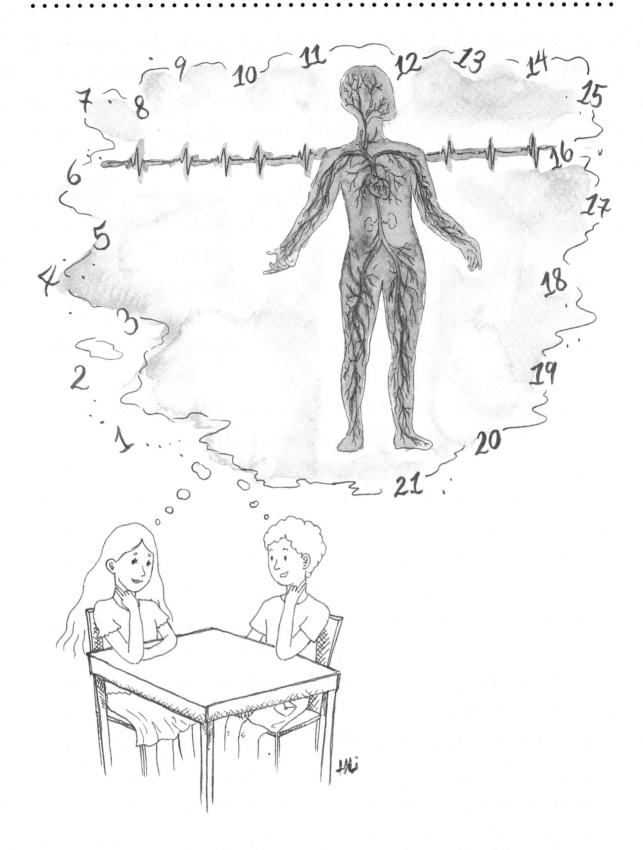

When I was in the sixth grade, our teacher taught us about the different organ systems of the human body. When we studied the circulatory system, we learned that the blood that flows through our bodies is *alive*. Our teacher showed us how the red and white blood cells, called corpuscles, circulate through our arteries and veins to bring oxygen and nourishment to, and to carry waste products away from, all the different parts of the body. She then told us to put our fingers on our necks very gently and take our pulse by counting our heartbeats. I'll never forget the first time I became aware of the rhythm of my own heartbeat.

As I took my own pulse, I could feel what was happening *inside* my body on the *outer surface* of my body. When I felt the beats of my own heart, I felt a conscious connection to the inside of myself as well as to the outside of myself, and I understood even more deeply that I was alive, both inside and out.

Our red blood cells contain hemoglobin, which is a protein composed in part of iron. Hemoglobin carries oxygen throughout our bodies. Like the hemoglobin in our red blood cells, the bricks that form our buildings are red because of the element of iron. Bricks are made of clay, and when the clay is fired in a kiln, the minerals absorb oxygen and they turn red.

Bricks are very strong, and they can bear a lot of heavy weight. Just as a brick building sits solidly on its foundation, a grounded person radiates a sense of physical power and emotional confidence when they stand firmly on their own two feet. This kind of power says,

> I am strong. I am capable. I am here. I am deeply rooted. I hold this space, not because anyone is challenging me, but because I just do. It's fun for me to feel this connection to the earth, and to my body, and to my own heartbeat.

Red is also the color of passion. One day I met a young man who worked with middle school students. When I asked him why he felt so passionately about his work as a teacher, the man told me how he often found himself standing up for his students. He explained how he provided these young people with a voice, and how he gave them a sense of strength that they could build on in their own lives. As he proudly told me:

I Stick With My Kids

I like to be a passionate person,
Someone who guides people in the right direction,
And who shows them the next steps forward.

I started thinking this way when I started teaching.
This was a few years ago.
I'm a middle school teacher.
I feel like those kids often have no voice,
And I help them to have a voice.

I love teaching because of the kids.
My students have taught me patience,
And how to take one step at a time,
And how to value life.

Red is my favorite color.
It brings me passion.
When I do something,
I put my whole heart and soul into it.
I'm passionate about my teaching.

Red is a very strong, passionate color.
That's why I always stick with red.
That's why I always stick with my kids.

Because I am also a teacher, I tend to meet a lot of teachers. When I work at my university, I not only get to meet other teachers and students. I also have the privilege of meeting people who come to campus to participate in research studies that take place in a very special robotics lab.[1]

These individuals are spinal cord injury patients. When they come to campus to work with researchers who are developing state-of-the-art robotics equipment, I sometimes get to sit with these individuals, and we talk about what matters the most in their lives.

One day I met a young man who had suffered a major spinal cord injury a few years prior. The young man now moved through the world with the aid of a wheelchair. He had an easygoing personality and a beautiful smile. When I asked him where he found his strength, the young man immediately started telling me about his family. His family had been by his side through everything, and they provided him with a foundational sense of strength and support. This strong sense of support enabled the young man to have a sense of curiosity and an openness to the unknown. When I asked him about the things that mattered to him, he warmly responded:

The Answer Could Be Anything

I love sports,
And I love being around family and friends.
I also like to work with my hands.
And I love learning.
Now, I find myself reading articles relating to my spinal cord injury,
And all the advances that they're making.
We're still trying to find things out.

The unknown is super interesting to me.
It's a puzzle.
I'm such a curious person.
I like to know things.
The answer could be anything.
It's interesting to see where we've been,
And where we're going.
This keeps your mind open to possibilities,
And open to so much.

What keeps me strong is hope.
If I choose not to be strong,
I'm choosing to live a solitary life.
There are so many things I want to do.
My only choice is to keep fighting.

My image now is of my whole family together,
All in the same place.
I wouldn't be where I am without my family.
Through thick and thin,
They have made me who I am.

Much like the bricks that hold up a tall building, this young man's family provided him with the building blocks of strength, grounding, and support. This solid underpinning gave the young man a special strength of heart, a sense of resilience, and an openness to explore the unknown with confidence.

Red is the color of such strength, power, and vitality. This kind of powerful life force is also anchored into the center of the earth. You can think of this vital energy as being like tomato juice, full of vitamins and minerals and nutrients. You can pull a lot of this energy up from the earth, through your body.

Just as you don't usually see the red blood inside of your body, you don't usually see the magma—or fiery molten rock—inside the earth's mantle, which is the layer that surrounds the planet's iron core. Sometimes you see volcanoes, which are like tubes that go down into the center of the earth and up into the sky. Volcanoes are named after Vulcan, the Roman god of fire, flames, and metalworking. Volcanoes are vents in the earth's crust that allow molten rock, gas, and steam to emerge. When a volcano erupts, the magma inside the earth flows up like a glowing red river. This fluid rock is called lava, and when it hardens, it helps to form the cone-shaped surface of the volcano.[2]

Volcanoes can appear not just in the earth, but also, in our lives. An emotionally explosive situation is called a volcano. Have you ever been so passionately angry that you were seeing red? Everyone has had this experience at one time or another. Children are often taught that it is not okay to be angry, and that their anger is bad. But there are times when your anger is good, because this emotional response can be telling you that you have a boundary, and that boundary has been crossed. The important thing is what you *do* with your anger. No matter how old you are, it is important to behave responsibly. This means that you want to be constructive with your anger, not destructive. When you are angry, it is time to breathe and move your body. It is time to run and dance and jump. It is time to take a pillow and hit the bed with it. These are big energies, and they want to move.

Red is the passion of this vital life force. It is the energy of resilience and the radiance within, like the magma of the earth, and the strength of the blood flowing through your body and your own beating heart.

Exercises for Experiential Learning, Visualization, and Reflection

- The color red can help you to experience your vitality in very concrete ways. One way to experience this is by taking your own pulse. Place the first and second fingers of your right hand on the inside of your left wrist, just below your thumb, and press in very gently. Then, count the beats of your own heart. As you do this, become aware of the inner rhythm of your own heartbeat. Reflect on the question of: How does it feel to consciously recognize a connection to an otherwise unseen life force that flows throughout my entire body, and which I can actually feel on the surface of my skin, in the pulse of my own heartbeat?
- The color red can also help you to envision many different types of vitality, strength, and stability. Have you ever practiced feeling connected to your own foundation? One way to do this is to stand up and consciously feel the connection between your legs and feet and the ground beneath you. You can also go outside and walk around the building you are in and notice the places where the architectural foundation touches the earth. Then go inside the building and consciously feel the connection between your feet, the floor below you, and the foundation underpinning the structure that houses you. You can reflect on questions such as: What do these structures have in common? How do they all

have the ability to bear weight and carry heavy loads? Why is it important to reflect on the subjects of strength, stability, and groundedness? How can being aware of these qualities enhance my own sense of support, balance, solidity, and resilience as I move through the world? How does this feel under normal circumstances? Why might these qualities be especially valuable when I'm facing challenging life situations?

- You can build on these themes as you contemplate the many different types of strength that you see in the world. What are these different strengths, and how do they relate to one another? How do they relate to the strengths that you perceive in yourself?

- Can you think of a historical figure, or a character in a book or a story, who exemplifies the qualities of strength, passion, vitality, responsibility, or resilience? Who is this figure, and why do you admire them?

- Was there ever a time when you or someone you know faced a hardship and had to be particularly resilient, in order to persevere through this difficulty or overcome a setback? What was the event, and how did you feel about it? What did you learn from this experience? Did it make you wiser or stronger? How so?

- Make a list of your own strengths and passions. What subjects do you have very strong feelings about? What stirs your own heart? What issues are you passionate about, and why do they move you so deeply?

- As you explore these questions, record your observations, images, feelings, and responses in a journal. Always date your journal entries and take note of any significant shifts in your thinking and the insights that emerge. As noted in the opening discussion, journals are private spaces that can be shared selectively, because your writings reflect fragments of your own mind and heart.

Notes

 1 Fancy Pants Reference Point: The robotics lab that I mention in this story is the MAHI (Mechatronics and Haptic Interfaces) Lab at Rice University, which is led by Professor Marcia O'Malley. Just as this lab focuses on "haptics for human performance augmentation", the innovative work performed in this space "focuses on the design, manufacture, and evaluation of mechatronic or robotic systems to model, rehabilitate, enhance or augment the human sensorimotor control system. To this end, we employ analytical and experimental approaches from the field of dynamic systems and controls, with inspiration from human motor

control and neuroscience." While working as a Literary Artist in this lab, I have had the privilege of hearing many inspirational stories as people reflect deeply on the nature of injury, impairment, rehabilitation, and empowerment. For more information on the MAHI Lab, see https://mahilab.rice.edu/.

 2 Fancy Pants Reference Point: When I'm looking for expert information, one of the sources I often turn to is the *Oxford English Dictionary* (or the *OED*, for short). This is not just one book, but an incredible collection of books that provides not only the definitions of words, but their origins (or etymologies), their meanings, and their usages. Looking at the *OED* is always an adventure worth taking. For more information on volcanoes, see the entry on this term in the *Oxford English Dictionary*, 2nd ed. (Oxford: Clarendon Press, 1989): https://www-oed-com.ezproxy .rice.edu/view/Entry/224428?rskey=ux6SUh&result=1&isAdvanced =false#eid.

Reference list

Simpson, J. A., and E. S. C. Weiner, eds. *The Oxford English Dictionary*. 2nd ed. Oxford: Clarendon Press, 1989.

Chapter 2: The School of Orange

Creativity, Empathy, Sensitivity, Emotional Expression, and Communication

Orange is the energy of childhood. This color evokes the warmth and creative energies of worldbuilding, as well as the qualities of sensitivity, empathy, and emotional expression. When you think of the color orange, you draw in creative life force. You can think of this color when you want to play, or when you radiate warmth and pleasure in whatever you are doing. Orange can be especially helpful in creating a sense of warmth when the world turns cold around you.

DOI: 10.4324/9781032613697-3

One day when I was in the third grade, the boiler at our school broke down. A boiler is a large vessel that helps keep a building warm. When the boiler broke down, we had no heat inside of the school, so all the children were sent home early, shortly after the school day began. It was the middle of winter in Connecticut, and it was *absolutely freezing* outside. There had been a big snowstorm just a few days before, and the snow was piled up high everywhere. While I was walking home, I got very cold from all the wet snow. When I came into the house, my hands and feet were freezing. After taking off my wet things in the cellar, I went upstairs to my grandmother's home.

In the house that I grew up in, my grandmother lived on the floor directly above us. I'll never forget coming into her kitchen on that very cold morning and seeing a silver saucepan with milk bubbling gently on the round orange burner of her kitchen stove. Everything was so welcoming and cozy that I immediately felt warmed, both inside and out.

Orange is the color of this warmth and creativity. I loved to watch my grandmother make beautiful things, especially homemade pasta. She would have all the ingredients lined up on her white enamel kitchen tabletop—flour, egg yolks, warm water, salt, and fresh parsley. Her tabletop was like an artist's palette as she made the dough and cut and shaped the pasta by hand. My grandmother could make something wonderful out of almost nothing.

One day I met an older woman who, like my grandmother, loved to cook special things for her family. Among the woman's culinary creations, her chocolate chip cookies were absolutely legendary. While this woman was very generous, and she would do almost anything for her loved ones, she absolutely **refused** to tell anyone the secret ingredient in her chocolate chip cookies. This intrigued me greatly, so of course, I had to give it a try. I walked right up to the woman and asked her about the cookies. Our conversation went something like this:

> Hi Mrs. Smith! How are you doing? You may not believe this, but everyone here is just buzzing about your famous chocolate chip cookies. You've got everyone guessing just what it is that you put into them. I don't suppose you could give me a tiny hint.

Guess what? No deal. Not even close. She was very polite about the whole thing, but no matter how clever or persuasive I was, she wasn't budging an inch. However, she did tell me:

The Secret Ingredient

My family is the sweetest.
And, the secret ingredient in my chocolate chip cookies is:
You have to put a lot of love in them.

I walked away thinking that "the secret ingredient" in the chocolate chip cookies was the woman herself, and the special way that she approached life, love, and creativity.

There are so many different ways to be creative. Perhaps you also like to cook. Or, maybe you are drawn to the visual arts—to painting and drawing, sculpture and photography. Maybe you like to sing or play a musical instrument. Maybe you enjoy fabrics and you like weaving and sewing, clothing and fashion, or interior decoration.[1] Maybe you like to build and fix things with your own hands. Perhaps you are one of those people who likes to work on cars, or who likes to work with metal or wood or mechanical things. There are so many different ways to be creative.[2] When you build a fort or draw a picture or tell a story, you can take people inside the world you create and you can share it with them, just like I'm sharing these stories with you.

One day I met a woman who loved to do wood carving. The woman described herself as a creative artist, and she told me about the house that she had built for herself with her own hands. Her story is called:

To Be Lifted

I am an artist.
I built my own house by hand.
I see patterns in the natural forms of the cedar wood.
One time I made porch railings from 4 x 6 boards.
I cut the boards into the shapes of feathers.
They made a good, stout railing,
But the porch looks like it's floating.

I see the world in a different way:
For what it can be.
For what's there to be appreciated,
And lifted.

There is so much beauty in this world,
And it's so easily overlooked.

I've always seen the world this way.
It's a choice,
To see the world
Through the eyes of an artist.

While this woman prided herself on her woodcarving and her carpentry, my grandmother was a creative artist with food and with the art of homemaking. If you were to imagine how it felt to be in my grandmother's kitchen, you would see a warm orange glow, bordering on peach and gold. Just sit with that color and keep it in your belly. Fill yourself up with it.

Just as orange radiates warmth and creativity, orange is a color of great sensitivity, emotional acuity, and a heightened capacity for listening and communication. This type of emotional power can help you cultivate a quality called empathy. Empathy is the ability to sense another person's feelings, thoughts, or ideas. Being empathic means that you may feel things in your gut, at the very center of your being. You may be an emotionally-centered person who is sensitive to other people's feelings, as well as to your own.

My grandmother knew how to create a sense of hospitality in her home, along with a feeling of comfort and safety. This made people feel warm and welcome, both inside and out. Because of the atmosphere that she created, many people would come to visit her. My aunts would often come in the afternoons to have tea. As a child, I would sit at the kitchen table and listen closely to their conversations. As I did this, I quickly realized that people were not only speaking through the words they said aloud. People were also speaking silently through the language of their eyes, in their tone of voice, in the way they carried their bodies, and how it felt to be around them. Everyone was talking silently in a language of energy and emotion, whether they were speaking out loud or not.

Empathy can make you a very good friend to someone because this emotional quality can help you understand another person's feelings and experiences. Sometimes it is very important to be able to put yourself in another person's place and to imagine how *they* feel about something, rather than just how *you* feel about something. Just because you feel a certain way doesn't mean that someone else will feel exactly the same way about the same subject. I'm sure you've seen many times when two people feel very differently about exactly the same subject.

Sensitivity and empathy are extremely valuable qualities because they can help you to relate to different people and to different aspects of life itself. Just as orange is an emotionally balanced color, the citrus fruit is both sweet and tart. Being able to see and taste the different sides of life is a great skill. You can think of this as a form of emotional gold. The word "orange" actually takes part of its name from the Latin word *aurum,* which means "gold".[3] Orange is the color of this emotional treasure.

Just as orange brings warmth to the body, this color is also full of a certain kind of emotional power. Orange can be the color of fearlessness. This color says, "I am unafraid". Sometimes we wear orange when we feel afraid, in order to have a bit of false bravado. We are in that false bravado because, in our hearts, we are very emotional beings. We are sensitive. Orange is the color of the power of that sensitivity.

Orange and blue are complementary colors. Together, they bring balance between your inner sensitivity and your inner power. Complementary colors relate to the visual arts and to color theory. Within the prismatic spectrum there are three primary colors: red, yellow, and blue. If you were to isolate one color (such as blue) and combine the other two (such as red and yellow), you would have the primary color (blue) and its complement (orange). Other complements include red and green, and yellow and violet. When you place the primary and the complementary colors next to one another, each color appears at its maximum intensity, and the colors complement and balance one another.

Orange can show you the many ways that *you* are an amazing creator. Just as orange is the warmth you feel when you come in from the cold, it is also the emotional warmth that you can share with others. Orange is the color of the radiant yellow-red that appears when pure gold is heated so that it can be molded and shaped into many beautiful forms. Orange is the color of this creativity, this warmth, and this emotional power.

Exercises for Experiential Learning, Visualization, and Reflection

- What do you love to create, and why? What is special about *your* creations? What makes them uniquely your own?
- Consider creating something special for the class and sharing the items as a group. How do people respond to each other's creations?
- Has there ever been a time when you experienced deep, heartfelt communication with another person? Where were you, and what were you doing? In this encounter, how did you and the other person use words, gestures, tone of voice, and the language of the eyes to communicate? Note the details of this experience in your journal.
- Can you recall a time when the feelings, facial expressions, and emotional energy that a person projected did *not* match the words that they spoke out loud? What was the situation, and how did you feel?
- Just as two people can feel very differently about the same subject, different colors can mean different things to different people. In some cultures, colors hold particular meanings, while in other cultures, the same colors hold very different associations. On an individual level, certain colors can evoke specific feelings and memories for one person, and very different meanings for someone else. The stories in this book provide just some ways to think about color. You can choose a particular color (such as orange) and, in your journal, you can reflect on questions such as: What does this color mean in the culture I live in? What might this color mean elsewhere in the world? What does this color mean to me? What might this color mean to someone else?

- Just as the color orange is very intimate and invites you to draw close, analyzing this shade also invites you to step back and take a broader, macro view of life. You can contemplate the big practical *and* philosophical questions of: What is being created within my communications, and what is being communicated within my creations?

- As this discussion shows, it is crucial to be in tune with your feelings. If you are feeling overwhelmed, or if you are having difficulty managing your emotions, or if you are experiencing high levels of stress or depression that interfere with your daily living activities, it is appropriate to seek adult and/or professional help. For many people, speaking with a counselor or participating in therapy are keys to maintaining good mental health.[4]

Notes

 1 Fancy Pants Reference Point: If you enjoy interior decorating and the applied arts, Leatrice Eiseman's book *Colors For Your Every Mood: Discover Your True Decorating Colors* (Sterling, VA: Capital Books, 1998) will be of interest. This book explores the influence of color in creating mood and atmosphere in interior decoration. Drawing on both high cultural and pop cultural reference points, the book discusses the historical uses of colors, their associated symbolism, and the various emotional responses that they can evoke, particularly within interior decorating schemes. While books like this can be whimsical and fun, it is important to remember that different colors can elicit very different responses from different people and that there is no single "right or wrong" approach to the responses that colors and emotions can hold for anyone.

 2 Fancy Pants Reference Point: Writing in *The New York Times*, Christina Caron discusses the ways in which practicing various art forms, such as creative writing, poetry, dancing, singing, or drawing, can improve mental well-being, as can partaking in activities such as visiting a museum or attending a concert. See Christina Caron, "How the Arts Can Benefit Your Mental Health (No Talent Required)," *The New York Times* (May 22, 2023): https://www.nytimes.com/2023/05/22/well/mind/art-mental-health.html. Educators Glenn Whitman and Ian Kelleher similarly observe that "One way students can create more enduring learning is by transferring knowledge into new mediums". For this reason, it is important to understand "the critical role of knowledge transfer through the arts, across all academic disciplines, as a tool for helping students

learn and remember content knowledge". See Glenn Whitman and Ian Kelleher, *Neuroteach: Brain Science and the Future of Education* (Lanham, MD: Rowman & Littlefield, 2016), p. 62.

 3 Fancy Pants Reference Point: If you were to look at the origins of the word "orange" in the *OED*, you would see references both to scent and to color, and you would have a very rich understanding of where this slice of language comes from. In particular, you would see: "auranja, fragrant; influenced by Anglo-Norman and Old French *or,* gold, with reference to the color. Similarly, post-classical Latin has *aurantia,* by association with classical Latin *aurum* gold". See the entry on "orange" in the *OED*: https://www-oed-com.ezproxy.rice.edu/viewdictionaryentry/Entry/132163.

 4 For an outline of mental health symptoms in children, adolescents, and adults, see the discussion formulated by Johns Hopkins Medicine, "Knowing When to Seek Treatment": https://www.hopkinsmedicine.org/health/treatment-tests-and-therapies/knowing-when-to-seek-treatment.

Reference list

Caron, Christina. "How the Arts Can Benefit Your Mental Health (No Talent Required)." *The New York Times,* May 22, 2023. https://www.nytimes.com/2023/05/22/well/mind/art-mental-health.html

Eiseman, Leatrice. *Colors For Your Every Mood: Discover Your True Decorating Colors.* Sterling, VA: Capital Books, 1998.

Simpson, J. A., and E. S. C. Weiner, eds. *The Oxford English Dictionary*. 2nd ed. Oxford: Clarendon Press, 1989.

Whitman, Glenn, and Ian Kelleher. *Neuroteach: Brain Science and the Future of Education.* Lanham, MD: Rowman & Littlefield, 2016.

Chapter 3: The School of Yellow

Self-Respect, Autonomy, Ethics, Innocence, and Vulnerability

The color yellow invites you to contemplate the public and the private aspects of yourself and others. This color is associated with self-respect, innocence, vulnerability, and sensitivity to ethical concerns. Yellow provides an opportunity to reflect on issues of presence, dignity, and self-esteem, and on the complex relations between an individual's inner and outer worlds.

When we move from orange to yellow, we move to softness. Yellow is the color of personal power and the innocence of new life. Yellow can show you how to use your strong will and self-determination to shine brightly and be your own

DOI: 10.4324/9781032613697-4

sun. Yellow brings an inner warmth, an inner glow, and an inner steadiness. This color is like a cat sleeping in a sunbeam. Yellow can be nurturing. It can be warm as we absorb it. It can fuel us in a balanced and whole way, where we don't feel like we have to push our will onto others. We can just be ourselves. We can sit easily in the sunbeam, like the cat, warm and content, without having to prove anything to anyone.

The qualities of self-containment and self-determination relate to the subject of autonomy.[1] Much like the color yellow, autonomy concerns the relations between the world inside of you and the world outside of you. To illustrate these concepts, I'll share a story of inner yellow, and then a story of outer yellow.

When I was a little girl, one afternoon my family went to visit my oldest cousin. He and his wife had just bought their first home. The house had a beautiful bay window that ran along the entire front wall of the living room. A bay window is a window that projects outward from the wall and creates a little recess or bay that you can sit in. This bay window had a cushioned bench that ran under the long row of window-panes that filled the entire room with so much sunlight. That afternoon, as the adults visited in the dining room, I sat quietly in the living room reading a book and look-ing out the bay window at the world all around me. Everything was so peaceful and

self-contained. I was inside the house, inside the window, and inside the bright yellow sunlight. I was deeply inside my own thoughts and content within myself. I was deep in my own interior yellow.

A few years later, I attended a very large public high school. The school auditorium had a big stage with deep burgundy curtains and a beautiful polished wooden floor. One of the highlights of the entire school year was the end-of-year show, where very talented students performed in front of the whole school. I'll never forget sitting in the audience, watching one young man sing. He was in the class just ahead of me, and he had an extremely sweet, strong voice. From the moment the curtains opened and the young man stepped onto the stage, everyone was charmed by his voice. When the song was over, he stood in the bright yellow spotlight, and everyone clapped very hard for a very long time. You could see the young man's eyes sparkle with pride as he smiled and bowed. This was his moment to be on the stage and to shine like the sun.

The sun is the central body of our solar system. It is the brightest object in the sky, and it is a powerful source of both light and heat. All of the planets orbit around the sun, and the position of the sun helps to determine the seasons. Just as life constantly shifts and changes, it is important to have a powerful inner center, a strong inner sun.

On earth, our sun is called Sol. Just as the word "solar" relates to the sun, it also refers to glory, joy, and good fortune.[2] The very name of the sun also calls to mind the idea of a solo—of performing alone, or of being on your own and "flying solo". To perform a solo is to do something all your own. During a solo, the person on the stage is the center of the performance and the star of the show.

Yellow is the color of the willpower that precedes such an accomplishment. There are times in life when you know what you want, you set a goal, and you pursue it. When you are in balanced yellow, you are in balanced will. You are exercising your autonomy. When you are in balanced will, you are in alignment with the power of your own inner sun.

At the center of your body is an area called the solar plexus. This is a network of nerves that converge in the abdomen. The solar plexus sits behind the stomach and below the diaphragm. Through the signals that the nerves send and receive, the brain stays connected to the abdominal organs. These organs are responsible for digestion—for absorbing and filtering food and drink—as well as for breathing, movement, and balance. The solar plexus is the gathering place of all of these powerful energies.

Just as the food that you eat and drink comes from living plants that grow in the bright sunlight, your solar plexus gathers tremendous energy from the sun. The solar plexus is like a powerful engine that sits at the very center of your body. When you sit in the bright yellow light of the morning sunlight, you can imagine your solar plexus at the pinnacle of its power, and you can begin to feel your own sense of willpower and self-determination.

Yellow is also the color of the sunrise and the new day. Yellow holds youthfulness and the budding of new life, like a budding yellow rose. This newness of life is like a new baby. A newborn's innocence and sweetness are almost dazzling. Everyone wants to look at the baby and hold it and feel its energy. It is like the sun peeking over the horizon. It is like something that came from the dark—that came from the mystery—and brought the light.

One day I met an older man who tenderly recalled how it felt to hold his daughters in his arms when they were newborn babies. As the man told me:

"Awesome" Doesn't Even Begin to Capture It

I was there when my daughters were born.
And I remember sitting there in a rocker,
With them bundled up in my arms,
With their fingers curled around mine.
The word "awesome" doesn't even begin to capture it.

Both of my daughters are beautiful.
But that wouldn't have made a bit of difference,
One way or the other.

Yellow is the color of innocence and play. Certain types of angels are called cherubs, and they often appear like playful children, with bright faces and glowing wings. Cherubs remind us of the joy and pleasure of childhood, and their color is a bright glowing yellow. Just as these presences hold the energy of innocence, they remind us that innocence is a great power that can easily be overlooked. Sometimes it can feel like a lost art to be in a state of innocence. To be innocent is to be vulnerable, without fear.

When you reflect on these subjects, you can also think about a very interesting paradox, namely: The youngest part of yourself is also the oldest part of yourself. Just think about this carefully for a moment. The very oldest part of you dates from the very first moment when you were born. This paradoxical image shows you how innocence and endurance, the new and the old, are not necessarily opposites, but how these seemingly opposite qualities can reside in exactly the same location.

Yellow is the color of this softness *and* this power. It is the color of wonder and inspiration, of new life and new energy, of self-esteem and self-determination. Think of the power of play in your life. Think of the power of self-determination in your life. Think of the power of newness in your life. Think of how the energy of new life inspires you. It opens your mind and brightens your heart and puts sparkles in your own eyes. Yellow is the softness and the radiance of this power. Yellow is the color of your own inner sun.

Exercises for Experiential Learning, Visualization, and Reflection

- Can you recall a time when you felt very peaceful and content just being on your own, flying solo, as it were? Where were you and what were you doing? How did it feel to be in your own company? What did you particularly enjoy about being on your own and being with yourself?

- Can you recall a time when you did something special that you were extremely proud of, and you shared this accomplishment with others? Where were you and what were you doing? How did this experience feel?

- What do you notice about yourself by looking at the private *and* the public experiences together? What aspects of your character remain consistent, and what qualities shift in these different circumstances?

- The color yellow also provides an opportunity to reflect on the extremely important subjects of ethics and values—of doing the courageous thing, especially when it is difficult to do so. Can you recall a time when you saw something that you knew wasn't right and you stood up for yourself or for someone else? What was the incident, and what did you do? How did this experience feel? How did others respond to you, and what did you learn?

- What are your own personal guidelines for determining right from wrong? Why is it important to have a personal sense of ethics?

Notes

 1 Fancy Pants Reference Point: Autonomy is a principle within Ethics. Ethics is the branch of philosophy that relates to various systems of power and value. Questions of autonomy directly inform a person's sense of their own boundaries, their personal and social values, and how they interact with and treat others.

 2 See the entry on "solar" in the *OED*: https://www-oed-com.ezproxy.rice .edu/view/Entry/184063?rskey=sJKkbY&result=2&isAdvanced=false #eid.

Reference list

Simpson, J. A., and E. S. C. Weiner, eds. *The Oxford English Dictionary*. 2nd ed. Oxford: Clarendon Press, 1989.

Chapter 4: The School of Green

Attunement to Living Systems and the Natural World

Located at the very center of the prismatic spectrum, the color green evokes a complementary sense of balance, abundance, gentleness, and power. The emotional keynotes include liveliness, vibrancy, growth, renewal, regeneration, and conscious attunement to living systems and the natural world.

Green brings in the energy of the earth. This is the energy of the rooted tree and the blossoming shrub. Green is the sense of abundance that is full of fruit, full of flowers, full of seeds, and full of nuts. Green is also the abundance that we bring into ourselves *and* that we give from ourselves. It is like a tree that takes in all the nutrients that it needs and then it makes acorns. It makes the seeds, the fruits, and the nuts for many, many to share. Green is the color of this abundance

DOI: 10.4324/9781032613697-5

coming into one, taking in all that it needs, and then giving forth for everyone to share, without any depletion.

The color green can feel like a gentle spring morning, or like the power of an endless summer day. The themes of power *and* gentleness arose the day that I spoke with a lovely woman who told me how, for her, green called to mind the bliss of

The Endless Day

My image is for all of my family—
My husband, my children,
All of my siblings, and my special friends—
To be together at a picnic.
We are just enjoying everything together.
I love the connection I have with my family and my friends.

The picnic is so carefree.
It is an endless day.
It makes me feel like living.
Green is my favorite color.
For me, green means life.

Just as green expresses the vitality of life, this color holds a tremendous sense of the blueprint of nature. There is so much power in a single seed. Every seed contains the knowledge of how to grow, how to live, and how to be.

When I was in the first grade, our teacher gave us each a small white paper cup and a few handfuls of soil. She told us to write our name on the bottom of the cup, and then she showed us some packets of seeds. There were seeds for pumpkins, squash, beets, and carrots. She let us each choose the seed that we wanted, and I chose the seed for sunflowers. Before I planted my seed, I looked at it very closely. I saw how the little black-and-white seed had stripes on its shell, and how it was round on one end and pointed on the other. The teacher told us to take our thumbs and make a hole in the dirt about one inch deep. Then we planted and watered our seeds, and we placed the cups on the windowsill that ran along one side of the classroom.

Each morning, I would look inside my paper cup to see if anything was happening. Even though I couldn't see it, something was *definitely* happening inside the cup. After a week or so had passed, a fresh yellow-green shoot had pushed its way up through the dark soil, and I knew that my sunflower was growing. Inside the paper cup, the ordinary little seed already had all of the information it needed for the plant to grow. The tiny black-and-white seed already held the blueprint for the entire sunflower.

As the other children's seeds sprouted, we could see the different shapes of the plants and the distinctive character of their leaves. And, even though this was a science lesson, every time I looked into the little paper cup, I felt like I was looking at magic.

Many people love plants, and they love to garden. One woman told me about the special garden that her father had planted on the rooftop of their tall city tower. The character of the garden shifted seasonally, as it reflected the blooming cycles of the various plants. As the woman recalled, the garden was always changing, and it was always very special. Because the garden looked different each time someone visited it, the garden showcased a fragile sense of beauty that you had to watch for very carefully. As the woman observed:

You Have to Catch Them, In the Moment

My father loved gardening.
He would buy special green plants for his garden.
His favorite plant has white flowers that only bloom once.
They are very rare,
And they are very beautiful,
So, you have to catch them,
In the moment.

Green plants may be growing in a garden in your own back yard, or on a windowsill inside your own home. Sometimes entire rooms of people's houses are dedicated to sunlight and to plants. A room with glass walls and a glass roof is called a conservatory or a solarium. When you walk into such a room, it always feels like you are outdoors, even though you are indoors.

When I went to college, a whole building was dedicated to the cultivation of plants. This is the Talcott Greenhouse at Mount Holyoke College in South Hadley, Massachusetts. Much like the windowsill of my first-grade classroom, the college greenhouse was—and still is—a very beautiful sunlit space that is also used for teaching purposes. As a student, I often visited the greenhouse because it was always so peaceful, and so full of life.

Just as green is the color of growth and new life, I think of this color in relation to the arts of both teaching and healing. In the classroom, a teacher will present you with new information, and then they will explain why these ideas matter. In the clinic, a healer will examine you and then they will explain why this information matters to you. All learning and all healing are transformational artforms. The knowledge that you gain in both settings can give you a sense of vibrancy, vitality, and attunement to life itself.

Green is also the color of community. Some cities have whole areas called greens. These are common places where people can meet and gather, and they are often located in the center of the town. Green is the color of the environment in small towns and in big cities, in great forests and in your own neighborhood.

Green is an extremely balanced color. This hue sits at the very center of the prismatic spectrum, between yellow and blue. Just as green balances the warm and the cool tones, it also balances a sense of power with a sense of gentleness. Green calls to mind the cycles of life and the seasons of nature. This color evokes both a lush summer and a mild winter, a time when you can still see green even though it is very cold outside. Focusing on green can help you attune to living systems and to the natural world. Green enables you to see the full spectrum of life itself, from states of fragility and vulnerability to passages of growth and strength.

If you have been ill and are feeling depleted, you can use the color green to bring in the energy of life and renewal. Just as green and red are complementary colors, together they bring in the energy of vitality. This is why the Christmas holidays are celebrations that bring in vital life force at a time of year when many people live in short days, filled with darkness and cold. During the holiday season, we often see the lush, dark green leaves and the bright red berries of holly, and the red and green foliage of poinsettias.

Green evokes a vital sense of new life. Just as green fruits and vegetables are not yet ripe, if you say that someone is green, this means that they are inexperienced and not yet developed. To be green is to be young and tender. It is to be fresh and full of hope.

One morning I was walking in Hermann Park, which is a large public park near my home in Houston, Texas. As I walked along the banks of a pond, I saw a group of Muscovy ducks. When you first see the ducks, you notice their bright orange and white faces, and their feathers appear to be very dark. But when you look more closely, you notice that their feathers are actually iridescent shades of green, blue, and brown. If something is iridescent, it means that the colors look like a rainbow—like soap bubbles shining in the sunlight.

Sometimes in life, ordinary things can be very special. This was one of those times. As I looked at the ducks more closely, I saw that they were new parents and that a group of tiny chicks sat in the shrubbery between the adults. The chicks all had golden faces with soft brown eyes and downy yellow and brown speckled feathers. A little while later, I chatted with the groundskeeper. This is the person responsible for maintaining that section of the park. When I told him about the chicks, the man told me about the joy people feel when they see the birds:

It's Real

People get amazed.
It's not a picture.
It's not a video.
It's real.

While the Muscovy ducks are wild birds that choose to make their home in the park, another man told me about the roosters and the hens that he had raised on his family farm when he was a boy. Reflecting on this childhood memory, the man poignantly told me how fond he was of

My Little Bird Family

I loved my little bird family,
And I miss my little roosters.
I had fifteen babies once.
The little bitty ones roamed around in the tall grass.
I was a boy,
And I had never had a little bird family like that before.
It was innocent,
And it was wonderful.

Green is the color of life moving forward. When you're riding in a car and you see a green light, you know that it is time to go, and you continue on your journey. Green is the color of this continuity.

Some trees are called evergreens because they don't ever shed their leaves, so they are always green. If something is evergreen, it means that it appears to be untouched by time. It is always fresh, always new, and always full of life.

Exercises for Experiential Learning, Visualization, and Reflection

- Invite a young child, or some young children, to grow a little windowsill garden, just as my First Grade teacher did with our class. Obtain some packets of flower and vegetable seeds, some potting soil, and some paper cups. Select plants that will feature different shapes and colors, so that the children can observe some variety as the seeds germinate. Invite each child to select a seed and to plant it with their own hands. Consider planting your own seed, as well. Then place the cups in a sunny windowsill. Visit the children regularly as you water the plants and watch the seeds grow. Make careful notes in your journal, not only regarding the progress and growth of the seeds, but of the children's emotional responses as they witness these processes of life. Also make careful notes regarding your own emotional and intellectual responses as you undertake this activity together.

- Either independently or as a group, make plans to spend time in nature. Visit a park or a green space, such as a community garden or a botanical garden, an arboretum, or a greenhouse. While you are there, consider how it feels to be around living green plants. Do you feel more vitalized and alive when you are surrounded by vibrant, growing plants?

- Choose a specific plant to focus on. Take a picture of the plant with your phone. If possible, gather a leaf or a flower, a seed or a nut. In your journal, consider: Which plant did you choose, and why were you drawn to it? What is the difference between being with a solid, green-leafed plant versus one with colored leaves or flowers? How do the different shapes, forms, and colors relate to one another? If possible, look up the Latin name of the plant. Do you see the plant's Latin name relating to its visible forms?

- Take some time to reflect on the relations that you perceive between individual plants and the larger landscapes that they inhabit. What do these living presences have in common, and how do they relate to one another? Put another way, what is the relationship between the microcosm and the macrocosm? How does it feel to be part of a living world?

- Just as green is a very balanced color, have you ever noticed how being in nature can be instantly calming to people? When you walk in a green space, you immediately calm down. Your eyes take it in. Your ears take it in. Your senses take it in, and you become peaceful. As a strategy of self-care, if you are feeling anxious, consider going out for a walk and drinking in the color green. Just breathe and allow the color to soothe you. It's like you're giving your mind and body a drink of something cool. Make notes in your journal about how this color feels to you.

Chapter 5: The School of Blue

Exploring Your Depths, Extending Your Heights, Expanding Your Power

The color blue can help you to cultivate an expanded sense of vision and intellect, of vulnerability and power. Blue is the color of the sky and the ocean. Just as the sky holds great heights and the water holds great depths, blue provides a means to envision vast spaces that are filled with immense power—much like the power of your own mind. Blue is like the Alpha and the Omega. These are the first and the last letters of the Greek alphabet. Blue can join the highest and the deepest, the first and the last. Just as the span of this color is immense, the power of this color is absolutely mind-blowing.

Blue can provide many ways for you to contemplate the great depths and the vastness within yourself. When I was a little girl, one of my father's best friends had a cottage by the shore in Old Saybrook, Connecticut, and we would visit him during the summertime. As a child, I had a lot of fun walking by the beach, playing in the sand, and collecting seashells. One of my most vivid memories is of standing at the edge of the water and looking out as far as my eyes

42

DOI: 10.4324/9781032613697-6

could see. As I gazed into the distance, I could see the place where the lighter blue of the sky met the darker blue of the water. At the very farthest point, the two colors blurred and merged to form an extremely vibrant blue line that was softer, brighter, and more intense than either of the two blues could ever be on their own.

As I stood at the edge of the shore, I was looking at the horizon line. The horizon is the place where the surfaces of the earth and the sky appear to meet, and one part of the world seems to touch another. The horizon is a soft boundary, a place of melting and fusion. Much like a sunbeam, you can see the horizon with your eyes, but you can't touch it with your hands.

The horizon is a place of paradox. Just as this zone separates *and* joins two parts of the world, the horizon is a point of boundaries *and* of connections. It is the place where the highest touches the deepest, and everything becomes brighter and more powerful together.

Even though I was only a little girl, as I stood on the beach that day, I began to imagine the idea of "forever". As I looked out at the horizon, I started to think about the beginnings and the ends of things, of who we are inside, and who we are before we are born, and who we might be after we leave. Even though I didn't yet have the language for it, I was thinking about the Alpha and the Omega. Looking out at the horizon taught me that I could look deep inside myself and imagine a place without boundaries—a place without beginning or end.

A few years later, our class took a field trip to The Breakers. This is the turn-of-the-century mansion that the industrialist Cornelius Vanderbilt built as a summer home in Newport, Rhode Island. Once again, I found myself standing at the edge of the water, although this time it was the Atlantic Ocean rather than the Long Island Sound. When we went inside to take a tour, the guide walked us through many beautiful rooms. At one point, we came to the formal dining room. This large room was filled with rich burgundy drapery, an enormous gleaming wooden table, and magnificent crystal chandeliers. While standing amidst all of this splendor, the guide told us to look straight up at the ceiling over the dining room table. On the ceiling, the artist had painted some soft white clouds floating over glowing patches of turquoise sky. This created the effect that people were dining outdoors, even though they were really eating indoors.

The term for this is *al fresco* painting, and it conveys a sense of being in the open air. When artists paint such optical illusions, the pictures are meant to fool the eye, which is why they are also called *trompe l'oeil* paintings. In these paintings, flat, two-dimensional surfaces appear to project forward and float in three-dimensional space. In a sense, through the paintings, artists take viewers into a different dimension.

I'll never forget the sense of amazement I felt while standing in the dining room at The Breakers, gazing up at the ceiling and seeing the sky in the house!

There are moments in life when familiar subjects appear in such strikingly novel ways that we can feel ourselves expanding. By presenting such an enlarging viewpoint, the dining room ceiling at The Breakers seemed to hold the unholdable. It seemed to hold the vastness of the sky inside the solid stone walls of the house.

Blue can give you a sense of vastness and expansiveness, as well as a feeling of inner peace and great power. One woman shared an exquisitely beautiful story of

The Blue That I Know

My image is of sitting on a beach, back home.
I'm watching the waves go by.
And, I'm just listening to them.
The waves come gently up to the shore,
And then they go back again.
The water is clear as crystal,
And you can dig your toes into the white sand.

There is a breeze,
And the air is clean and clear.
This gives me a sense of peace.
That's why this is so meaningful.
I feel so much peace at the beach.
I feel a closeness to creation.

This scene is blue, sky blue.
That light blue is so peaceful, and so calm.
I look out at the horizon,
Where the sky meets the water,
And I want to be
In that blue that I know.

While this woman's story is very calm and gentle, for other people, the color blue can represent great power and freedom. As one man wisely observed:

The Ocean Is Not Just One Color

Blue water is very tranquil.
It gives me great serenity.
It could be a dark blue or a light blue.
When you're at the ocean
You can work with all of the blues.
I've been playing around with images
That express this type of freedom.
When you do this, you can always remember:
The ocean is not just one color.

The color blue is expansive enough to hold everything. Because blue has the potential to hold everything, this color is associated with truth and loyalty. Maybe you've heard someone describing a good friend as "true blue"? To be loyal is to be faithful, including faithful to the truth. Sometimes it is important to be able to see difficult things, especially when they are true. Blue can help you to find the clarity and the courage to see the bigger picture. Just as blue radiates truth, it can knock out all that is untruth.

Just as blue is the color of truth, it can also provide a powerful shield of protection. There are times when you want to open up and expand your horizons, like the times that I looked out at the ocean or up at the ceiling. And then, there are times when you want to pull in and feel safe and contained. Just as the horizon marks a boundary, it also sets a limit. Blue is the color of this protection, and you can use the sky as your shield.

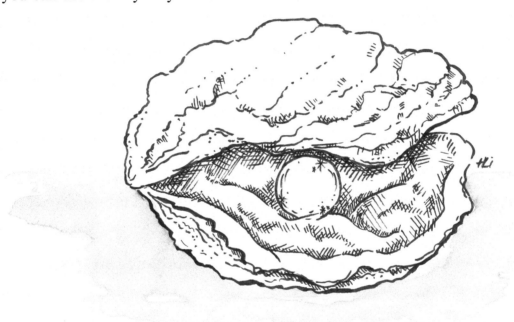

As a way to show care for yourself, when you are frightened, you can always shield yourself with the color blue. When the world becomes overwhelming, you can call in the blue light. It can be a soft blue light or a strong blue light. It doesn't really matter which one you choose. You can surround yourself in a blue bubble, or place yourself in a column of blue light. You can always say,

> I feel overwhelmed. I'm going to put this blue light all around myself, simply to feel better, calmer, more soothed and protected. Then I can feel like the world is all mine. I can feel like I am only responsible for myself. I do not need to fix anyone else. I do not need to take on anyone else's issues. I can just be me.

And then, you can feel like the world is *your* oyster.

Exercises for Experiential Learning, Visualization, and Reflection

- Either independently or as a class, make plans to visit an art museum or a historic house. While you are there, select an artwork that you are particularly drawn to, preferably a piece that feels expansive. Then consider: What piece did you select, and why were you drawn to it? How do you feel when you are in the presence of the artwork, and how do you feel when you step away from it? What shifts in you as you move between the rooms or galleries?
- Either independently or as a class, make plans to visit a body of water, such as an ocean, a lake, or a pond. Gaze at the farthest point of the horizon line and extend your gaze and your thoughts laterally, out across the field. Ask yourself: How do my eyes and my mind fill in the space between these distant points? Does it feel like I am stretching, with my eyes and with my mind?
- As you consciously feel your gaze and your thoughts expand, make notes in your journal regarding: How do these experiences feel? How and where can I apply these insights to other areas of my life? How can I consciously incorporate this sense of expansion and depth inside of myself?

- Just as the horizon can be a very powerful place of self-exploration, blue is a place where you can think your deepest thoughts. What are the deepest places inside of you? What are the highest places inside of you? Just as two parts of the world meet and join at the horizon line, there are different places inside of you where one realm touches another. How do you begin to envision your own horizons?

- Look up at the sky and consciously feel your mind expanding as you stretch your gaze upward. Pay careful attention to how you feel. Do you feel more elevated and expansive as you look up?

- Now look down at the ground below you. What do you notice as your gaze travels downward? What can you see that is not ordinarily visible?

- Now bring your gaze back to a level position and ask yourself: What does it mean to have a panoramic perspective? Do you feel "larger" as your eyes and mind take in the world all around you? What do you notice, and how does this feel?

- Finally, put the different perspectives together and ask yourself: Why is it important to be consciously aware of where you are standing and what you are seeing? Why is it important to be able to go high, to go deep, and to gaze panoramically? How does it feel to have such an enlarged and enlarging viewpoint?

- The next time you are frightened or feeling overwhelmed, imagine shielding yourself with the color blue. Imagine surrounding yourself with a soft blue light or a strong blue light. Then notice how you feel, and note your responses in your journal.

Chapter 6: The School of Indigo

Shadows, Doublings, Dreams, Fairy Tales, and the Subconscious

Just as the color blue allows you to explore external vision, indigo provides a wonderful counterpart because this color relates to inner vision and subtle intelligence. Indigo can show you the hidden dimensions of your own mind and imagination. This color can be your guide to the realms of twilight and secrets. Just as indigo sheds important light on shadows and the subconscious, this color illuminates subjects that might otherwise remain hidden.

Indigo is the color of magic and mystery. Indigo relates to secret places, and this color can move into the shadows very quickly and with great purpose. It can do this almost unseen, almost unknown. In the shadows, indigo can find what is needed and bring it back out into the light. This color has tremendous power, but it is not often sought or understood. Indigo is like a doorway between blue and violet, and truly, it can be a doorway into other realms.

If I were to tell you a fairy tale, it might begin with an image of a child walking through a forest at twilight, when the sky is moving to indigo. Indigo can be like the feeling you have when you have lost your way and you need something to help light your path.

When you think of indigo, you can think of will-o'-the-wisps. Will-o'-the-wisps are in the fairy tradition. They are little lights that light your way in the dark.[1] In many stories, will-o'-the-wisps lead people astray by seeming to encourage them when they are actually misleading them. Will-o'-the-wisps are known for being hard to catch and nearly impossible to pin down. They can be pesky and take you on a path that gets you lost, or they can be extremely helpful and light up a path that takes you where you need to go.

DOI: 10.4324/9781032613697-7

Sometimes will-o'-the-wisps can lead you home. You can think of "home" as more than just a physical place, like the house that you live in. Home can also be a place deep inside of yourself. It can be the part of your mind that believes in magical creatures like will-o'-the-wisps. You might hear such a fairy story and think, "Oh, there are beings that live in another dimension that I cannot see? Of course there are! They are magical? Of course they are! Sometimes they bridge the dimensions and I can see them? Of course I can!"

Indigo relates to the part of your mind that believes in magic. This color can take you to in-between places. Just as indigo holds the place between blue and violet, you can think of indigo as the place in your mind where you can see different realms and meet different parts of yourself.

One day I met a woman who told me an extremely beautiful story about the day she and her children visited a natural landscape—and how it felt like they were all entering a magical realm, a kind of fairy world. As the woman recalled this amazing landscape, she marveled at how

It All Came From a Rock That Is Cracked

When my kids and I were traveling and sight-seeing,
We got to be around nature and natural waterfalls.
We hiked and crawled up the sides of mountains,
And we found some little pools to swim in.

This was a ridiculously good trip.
It was so relaxing.
We got to visit places where no one else has gone.
It was like a fairyland.

This trip felt like it was private,
And like the waterfalls were all ours.
No one else was there,
And it was very peaceful.

Pools of water came down in little falls.
It was cool, fresh mountain water,
Coming down over your entire body.
It was very cleansing and comforting,
Letting the water wash over you like this.

The waterfalls were so beautiful.
It was a shining day.
And it all came out of
A rock that is cracked.

Indigo can lead you to in-between spaces—to half-hidden places that are full of magic—so that you can see the world in a new light. There are so many different ways to walk through an indigo doorway. Another way is to walk outside at twilight. Twilight arises at both dawn and dusk. Twilight is a hinge point between day and night, and it holds aspects of both rising and falling light. When you think about twilight, you can ask yourself a magical question, namely: "What does it mean to see in two lights?" Twilight is literally a time of doubled light ("twi-light").[2]

Much like twilight, the color indigo is associated with in-between times and places. These liminal spaces can appear like gateways to other states of mind and being. Points of entry into these otherwise unseen worlds can include dreams and fairy tales, silhouettes and shadows, and the conscious act of closing your eyes in order to see in the dark, and to see in secret.[3]

There are so many different ways to see life differently. In addition to walking in the dusk of twilight, you can go outside in the bright sunlight and study your own shadow. Have you ever done this?

When I was in middle school, one morning I spent an entire recess period playing with my own shadow. I looked very closely and saw how it was attached to my feet and how it mirrored my silhouette. I watched how my shadow moved as I moved, as I walked or jumped or ran. This experience was very powerful because it helped me to see myself in a completely new light. I understood that there was another part of myself that was always there, even if I couldn't always see it. I literally saw myself in two lights—not at twilight, but in broad daylight.

There is a part of your mind that is as quiet as a shadow. This part is like a good friend and a wise counselor who knows many, many things. Sometimes when people close their outer eyes and look at the world with their inner eyes, they can see the secret parts of life, and they gain insight into *why* people do the things that they do. Paradoxically, sometimes you have to close your eyes in order to see. This can be especially helpful when you want to see *into* a situation, rather than when you just want to look at the outer surfaces of things.

There is a part of your mind that you know when you are awake, and there is another part of your mind that arises in the dreamtime. When you are awake, your mind brings you awareness and knowledge. This part of your mind is called your consciousness. This part has great purpose and intent, and it is the part of your personality that you know very well. But when you go to sleep, the subconscious part of your mind arises. This part lies just below or beyond what you know when you are awake. This part of your mind is instinctive and intuitive, and it can influence how you feel about life, and how you react to things.

The subconscious part of your mind is associated with dreams. Dreams are the thoughts, feelings, and images that your mind generates while you are asleep. Sometimes dreams are like stories. Dreams can also bring you awareness of things that you couldn't see otherwise.

Indigo sits in the creative space of dreams and memories. This color is associated with the wisdom of the fairy world and the vastness of the dark night skies. One woman told me an indigo story as she recalled

The Stars Right Over My Head

My image is of a little girl in fairyland.
This is really a peaceful forest with butterflies and deer coming by,
And a house with a water well.

My grandparents lived in an old house in the middle of the forest.
It was red limestone, very cute and very narrow.
It was like fairyland.

I had very special moments there.
My happiest memories are of being there,
With me and my brother playing in the forest.
It was like a big playground, and very idyllic.
We just laughed and played all day.

I was very close to both of my grandparents.
My grandpa was one of the most wonderful grandpas.
He sat in a big chair, with a pipe in his mouth.
My grandmother was a very loving person.
When you woke up in the morning, breakfast was always ready.

This place is not something that I can see and touch now.
It's somewhere I can go in my mind,
And it makes me feel happy.

My brother and I shared a little room
In the attic of the house.
The attic was magical.
There was a little window in the ceiling,
And I could look through the window at night
And see the cats tiptoeing around outside.
And I could see the stars,
Right over my head.

At the end of the day, when darkness comes, you can always close your eyes and tell yourself, "It's time to climb into bed with the indigo light". Indigo is sleeping time. It is the time when your brain integrates all of the information it has learned throughout the day. So much information comes in from all the senses, from the mind, and from the emotions. In the sleep time, the information integrates like a filing cabinet in your brain and the world comes into balanced order. The dreamtime is for bringing order to your brain. Your brain works very hard while it is resting, both to make sense of the world and to play.

With indigo, there is no need to be afraid of the dark, or fearful of the shadows. Indigo can fill you with new insights and new constellations of ideas. The dream-time is a time for letting your brain explore other realms. As you go to sleep, you can tell yourself, "It is time to visit the night sky. It is time to visit the stars. It is time to visit the moon and the indigo sky".

Indigo is the color where magic happens.

Exercises for Experiential Learning, Visualization, and Reflection

- Go out into the bright sunlight and study your own shadow. Make notes regarding the rhythms of your gait and the distinctive forms of your silhouette. How does your body move? What are your own kinetic observations? That is, what do you notice about your own body in motion? What is distinctive about *your* shadow, including your silhouette, and your style of walking and running and moving through the world? What does examining your shadow enable you to see that you couldn't ordinarily see? Why is it important to reflect thoughtfully on how you move through the world? What does this teach you about yourself?

- Consider writing your own fairy tale. It might begin with an image of a child walking through a forest at twilight when the sky is moving to indigo. The child may have lost their way, and they are looking for something to help light up their path. What appears to the child, and where does the path lead them? How is the fairy world that you create in your mind both similar to, and different from, the everyday world that you see all around you?

- Consider keeping a dream journal to gain insight into the otherwise hidden aspects of your mind. What do your dreams show you? How and why is it important to know the hidden parts of yourself, as well as the obvious ones?

- Another way to see life differently is to sit quietly and look at the world with your eyes closed. You can see the world in a different light when you connect with your intuitive self. Intuition is a deep, instinctive, inner knowing. Have you ever sat in a quiet place, closed your eyes, and viewed the world in a different light? What did you see, and what did you learn? Practice this exercise in light of what you have learned about the color indigo.

- Consider the bigger picture of the mind and the psyche by asking yourself these questions: Why is it important for me to know my presence in both the lights and in the shadows? What do these domains have in common, and how are they different? Why is this information valuable, and why does this knowledge matter to me?

Notes

1 Fancy Pants Reference Point: Will-o'-the-wisps are associated not only with fairy stories, but with certain natural phenomena, such as the phosphorescent lights that appear to float over bogs or marshy grounds at night. They are also associated with colonies of bacteria that become visible after a rainstorm. The latter include the "gelatinous colonies of cyanobacteria of the genus *Nostoc*". See the entry on "will-o'-the-wisp" in the *OED*: https://www-oed-com.ezproxy.rice.edu/viewdictionaryentry/Entry/229084.

2 Fancy Pants Reference Point: The etymology of the word "twilight" is suffused with paradox. The prefix "twi" is related to the German word *zwei*, which denotes not only the numerical value of two but the analogical concepts of doubling, doubled, and twice. Thus, twilight is a simultaneous juncture of two distinctive lights, just as it is a hinge between the diurnal and the nocturnal realms.

 3 Fancy Pants Reference Point: One of the most complex and intriguing discussions of what it can mean to "see in secret" can be found in the philosopher Jacques Derrida's reflections on the singularity and uniqueness of every human being. One day, you may want to read about these subjects in Jacques Derrida's book *The Gift of Death*, trans. David Wills, 2nd ed. (Chicago: University of Chicago Press, 2008). If you like this book, then you'll *love* his museum-based volume *Memoirs of the Blind: The Self-Portrait and Other Ruins*, trans. Pascale-Anne Brault (Chicago: University of Chicago Press, 1993).

Reference list

Derrida, Jacques. *The Gift of Death*. Translated by David Wills. 2nd ed. Chicago: University of Chicago Press, 2008.

———. *Memoirs of the Blind: The Self-Portrait and Other Ruins*. Translated by Pascale-Anne Brault. Chicago: University of Chicago Press, 1993.

Simpson, J. A., and E. S. C. Weiner, eds. *The Oxford English Dictionary*. 2nd ed. Oxford: Clarendon Press, 1989.

Chapter 7: The School of Violet

Growth and Change, Transformation and Manifestation

From indigo, we move to violet. Violet is truly the color of kings and queens. Violet evokes images of royalty and sovereignty, of great power and self-determination. Violet can help you to face your fears so that you can grow and transcend your previous limitations. This color holds the powers of transformation and manifestation. These are the abilities to make changes, to make things up, and to make them real. Violet can assist you with setting and attaining goals, and with fostering the capacity for growth and change.

DOI: 10.4324/9781032613697-8

The Royalty of old liked to wear violet robes because this color made them look regal. Both historically and in today's world, kings and queens are called Sovereigns. To be sovereign is to be free from outside control, and to be independent within one's own domain. Sometimes in life it is necessary to make important changes in order to be free and to be sovereign. Violet is the color of this transformative power.

I once met a woman who told me an extraordinary story about a castle. History literally came alive for this woman in a very real and personal way. While her story might sound like a fairy tale, it is a true story of personal transformation, and of how doing historical research both informed and elevated the woman's understanding of herself and her life. As she told me:

It Was Just Magical

I have always been drawn to Switzerland,
And I never knew why.
I had seen pictures in calendars,
And I decided to go.

The mountains and the lakes are gorgeous.
The villages are so cute.
When you hear the bells on the cows,
It's just magical.
The first time I went,
I felt like I was home.

I did some research on my family history,
And I discovered a link with my own ancestry.
It was very weird because,
I had always been told that my family was Celtic.
But, looking at the history of my maiden name,
I saw that it had been corrupted.
In Switzerland, I found a castle with my uncorrupted family name.
This made me understand why I felt such a deep connection there.

I am so thankful that I was able to see this.
It is a beauty beyond what you see every day.

I have always liked history,
And to be able to connect myself to this history—
It was just magical.

Violet is filled with such magical powers of transformation. While the woman shared a powerful story of self-discovery, we can also examine transformation from a very different point of view:

Have you ever had to do something that you were really, really scared to do? In the summer between eighth and ninth grade, I started volunteering at the local hospital. My mother saw an ad for the hospital's volunteer program in the newspaper, and she thought it would be a good idea if I gave it a try. She was absolutely right!

When I first heard about the hospital's volunteer program, a part of me was super-excited and absolutely fascinated. This part of me deeply wanted to participate in the program. Yet, another part of me was totally terrified. I had always been frightened of medical things, and I wasn't sure how much pain or suffering I would see if I worked in a hospital. On the day of the training, I was so nervous that I accidently poured tea rather than milk into my father's hot coffee! At the end of the afternoon, the volunteers were taken on a tour of the hospital buildings so that we could see the different departments where we could work. While we were walking down the long white hospital corridors, I became so anxious that I actually felt dizzy!

Fortunately, that awful feeling passed quickly. As soon as my actual work began, I completely forgot about myself, and I started to focus on other people. This experience was both freeing and transformative. It taught me that changing one's focus can be like magic. This shift in my perspective enabled me to spend the next two years working in the hospital's Pediatrics Department, where I learned an enormous amount about myself and the power that comes from caring for others. I would not trade these experiences for anything in the world.

Sometimes in life, it is necessary to do something extremely difficult in order to make important changes. Making these changes is another way that you can grow and show care for yourself. As a young teenager, I learned that I had to let go of something that I *didn't* want in order to create space for something that I *did* want. This experience was not only transformative; it was transcendent. To transcend something means to rise above or go beyond a limit or a boundary.

You have probably heard of people ascending a mountain (scaling up), or of descending a mountain (climbing down). But have you ever heard of someone transcending a mountain? Transcendence is like climbing across a steep mountain, while continually rising from one ridge to the next. Eventually, you climb so high that you reach a place where you can see farther than you've ever seen before.

Transcendence is sometimes associated with manifestation—creating something new. People often think of manifestation as being like a magician pulling a rabbit out of a tall black silk hat. You can think of manifestation as a creative power deep within yourself. This power is important when there is something inside of you that you want to change, like the way I wanted to change my fear of working in a hospital.

It can take a lot of courage to make important changes so that you can live your life differently. Sometimes it takes great courage to say, "I'm going to fight for this, even though it is uncomfortable". This type of self-overcoming represents a

form of self-mastery. When you use your power to face your fear and to create something new and wonderful, you are practicing a form of sovereignty. You are learning how to be your own master, your own king or queen.

But before you can climb up, you first have to recognize that you are standing in a lower place and that you want to climb higher. This takes both self-awareness and a degree of humbleness that allows for humility. Humility is the ability to recognize your own limitations. It is about being modest enough to see that there is always so much more to see. Humility is also about being able to see the value of things that might otherwise appear lowly and be overlooked.

I'm now going to teach you a magical paradox: *Sometimes in life you need to be small in order to become large.* Humility is a kind of superpower that is linked to transformation. Sometimes the kings and queens of old walked among their people disguised as peasants. Their humble appearance allowed them to go anywhere without calling attention to themselves. As they walked freely throughout their kingdom, they could see life far more fully and know things far more deeply than they ever could if they had only sat comfortably on their thrones in their splendid violet robes. The important lesson is: humility and strength are *not* opposites. They are two sides of transformative power. (Just trust me on this; I know what I'm talking about.)

Just as violet is associated with royalty, this flower is very sweet and modest. Violets can be purple, blue, or white, and they usually have tiny bits of gold sitting like small crowns at their centers. The plants are very humble, and they are also very tenacious. This means that they know how to hold their ground and blossom in the shade. Just as violets don't always have to be in the bright sunlight, the plants are so common that sometimes people don't even notice them. Whenever I see violets, I always think of scattered royalty holding court among the shadows.

The color violet is associated with an expanded sense of vision and communication. Violet can teach you how to see the world in an entirely different light. In nature, there are certain colors that human beings can see with their regular eyesight, and there are colors that lie beyond the far ends of the visible spectrum. These colors are called infrared and ultraviolet.[1]

While you might not be able to see these colors, some insects and animals can.[2] Sometimes people use cameras fitted with special lenses and filters in order to see in ultraviolet light. Indeed, some plants and animals look one way when seen in familiar light conditions, and they look extremely different when seen in ultraviolet light. If you were to look at certain flowers in this light, you would see how the plants communicate with insects through the enhanced patterns that appear on their petals. This makes it easier for creatures such as bees and butterflies to identify the flowers from a distance. Perhaps you can also relate to the idea of seeing the world differently, like a butterfly or a bee?

Black-eyed Susan
Seen in regular vision

Black-eyed Susan
seen in ultraviolet light

Violet allows you to see the world in many different lights, and to recognize that everyone sees the world in a slightly different way. Violet helps you to recognize that every person is unique and powerful, and that everyone is a sovereign being. In this way, everyone is like a king or a queen. Violet can help you to see the nobility of everyone, especially yourself.

Exercises for Experiential Learning, Visualization, and Reflection

- Can you recall a time when you faced a fear or made a meaningful change? What was this experience, and how did you feel? Who were you before and after you made this change?

- Can you identify something in your life now that you would like to change? How might you go about doing so? How does creating positive change help you to grow and attain more self-mastery? How does this relate to your own sense of power?

- Certain fish and insects, as well as cold-blooded animals like snakes and frogs, can see infrared light as bodies give off heat. In turn, birds, bees, butterflies, and some reindeer can see the enhanced patterns of plants in ultraviolet light. If you would like to see this for yourself, you can view Don Komarechka's five-minute YouTube video, "Ultraviolet Light Explained: See the world through the eyes of insects" at: https://www.youtube.com/watch?v=2gduA3EM26M.

  After viewing the video, consider how it might feel to view the world differently, like a butterfly or a bee. Does this idea of expanded vision appeal to you? Why?

- Can you think of someone in your life who is very modest and humble, a person who inspires and supports others, and who places other people's achievements ahead of their own? Who is this person, and why do you admire them? Have you ever told this person that you recognize the power of their humility and that you are grateful for their presence in your life?

- Contemplate the nobility of everyone, including yourself. What does this quality look like in yourself and in others, and how does it feel?

Notes

1 Fancy Pants Reference Point: Infrared is the invisible electromagnetic radiation that lies beyond the red end of the spectrum, and ultraviolet is the invisible electromagnetic radiation that lies beyond the violet end of the spectrum. See the definitions of "infrared" and "ultraviolet" in the *OED:* https://www-oed-com.ezproxy.rice.edu/view/Entry/95621?redirectedFrom=infrared#eid and https://www-oed-com.ezproxy.rice.edu/view/Entry/208724?redirectedFrom=ultra+violet#eid.

2 Fancy Pants Reference Point: For more information on these subjects, see Didem Tali, "Animals That Can See Infrared Light", *Sciencing.com* (June 25, 2022): https://sciencing.com/animals-good-night-vision-8100479.html; and Rebecca J. Rosen, "Animals that Can See or Glow in Ultraviolet Light", *The Atlantic* (August 15, 2011): https://www.theatlantic.com/technology/archive/2011/08/6-animals-that-can-see-or-glow-in-ultraviolet-light/243634/6.

Reference list

Rosen, Rebecca J. "Animals That Can See or Glow in Ultraviolet Light." *The Atlantic,* August 15, 2011. https://www.theatlantic.com/technology/archive/2011/08/6-animals-that-can-see-or-glow-in-ultraviolet-light/243634/6.

Simpson, J. A., and E. S. C. Weiner, eds. *The Oxford English Dictionary*. 2nd ed. Oxford: Clarendon Press, 1989.

Tali, Didem. "Animals That Can See Infrared Light." *Sciencing.com,* June 25, 2022. https://sciencing.com/animals-good-night-vision-8100479.html.

Chapter 8: The School of Silver

The Visionary Qualities of Alchemy and Reflection

Silver is a teacher of great cleaning and cleansing, of great value and reflection. Like copper and nickel, silver is one of the basic chemical elements of the earth. Silver is an excellent conductor of heat, electricity, and sound. That is why some musical instruments are made out of silver, and why silver flutes give such a clear, bright, melodious sound. When silver is polished, its lustrous surface provides a clear reflection, like a mirror. Silver is used in coins, and it is a valuable commodity that can be bought and sold, much like gold, wheat, or coffee. Silver is soft and malleable enough to be formed into many complex shapes, such as plates and jewelry and silverware. This precious metal is versatile and elegant, and it is seen in both everyday use and on special occasions.

DOI: 10.4324/9781032613697-9

To explore the special qualities of silver, I'm going to tell you a true magical story about a little silver coffee pot. But first, I have to tell you about the circumstances in which the story arose. For many years I have worked, not only in universities and museums, but also in hospitals. In hospitals, I often work with people who are extremely ill and facing the very end of their lives.[1] At this special time of life, people will often tell stories about what matters the most to them. Because the stories reflect the wisdom of people's life experiences, they are filled with the vibrancy of life itself, and with many valuable insights on the different types of love that we experience as human beings. As people speak, I write down their words exactly as they state them, and I put their phrases into successive lines that resemble poetry. I then give the stories back to the person, as a gift for themselves and their family. You have already read several of these stories in *The Colors of Life*. Here is another one, which will show you the special qualities of silver.

Once upon a time, people made coffee in little metal coffee pots that sat on their kitchen stovetops. Almost everyone had a little silver coffee pot, and this was often the very first thing you saw when you walked through someone's kitchen door. The coffeepots had round metal bodies with clear glass buttons on their lids. The buttons were actually little windows that allowed you to look inside and see the coffee perking as it brewed.

One day I met an older couple who had been married for many, many decades. As we visited, the couple reflected on the life they had built together. The woman in the hospital bed smiled as she told me about how, when she and her husband were first married, they lived in a tenement building in New York City. A tenement is a tall city building that holds many apartments, where many families live. The woman described her family as humble people who had worked very hard for all they had in life. As the woman spoke, I arranged her words into a poem as a gift for her and her husband. Now, the story is a gift to all of us. As the woman told me:

I Still Have That Coffeepot

My husband and I have had many years of marriage.
We are both originally from Italy.
At first, we lived in New York City,
In a tenement building.
My husband was always there for me then,
And he's always here for me now.

When we got married,
We started out with two knives, two forks,
A cooking pot without a lid,
And a $1.50 coffee pot.
It's funny what you remember.

My husband is honest and hardworking.
He's helped a lot of people.
He's the best thing in my life.
And, I still have that coffee pot.

This story is all about the value of presence. No matter what happened in the couple's daily life, the little silver coffee pot was on their table every morning as they ate breakfast together. Because the little silver coffee pot was always there, it held far more than coffee. It also held all of the memories of the experiences that the couple shared through their long life together. And now, the woman was thinking about these memories with so much love at the end of her life.

If you didn't know the story, you might look at the little silver coffee pot and only see an ordinary object with no special value at all. But now that you've heard the story, you can see so much more. You can see how something that seems to have little to no value to one person can hold enormous value and meaning for someone else.

This story reflects a magical paradox because two seemingly opposite states are true at the same time. That is, the little silver coffee pot is very commonplace *and* it is very special. It is both cheap and valuable. It is very small, and yet it is very large. It is both ordinary and mystical. It is an empty vessel that overflows with a lifetime's worth of meanings. And now that you've heard the story, you may never look at life—or at a coffee pot—the same way again.

Yet, there is still more to see. The little silver coffee pot can also be approached as a kind of mirror. Just as its shiny surface reflected whatever went on in the couple's daily life, their story shows you how the things that we value the most can have a protective feeling for us. Silver is a powerful color of protection. Along with bronze, iron, and steel, silver was used historically in the crafting of body armor. You can always think of silver as being helpful in your own personal shielding. If you have to face a particularly difficult situation, you can always imagine yourself wearing a silver bulletproof vest. You can think of this as a silver shield that provides you with great strength, just as it protects your own tender heart.

The little silver coffee pot also teaches the power of transformation. As you begin to look at life differently, life will appear differently before your eyes. As the world appears in a new light, *you* change too, and a new light appears in your own eyes, as well. Silver is an excellent mirror for reflecting these changes. A mirror is a smooth surface that reflects a clear image of something. In olden times, mirrors were made out of polished metal. Today, mirrors are made of glass, and their backs often have a reflective silver coating.

Silver is not only a color of great reflection; it is also a color of great alchemy. Alchemy is associated with magic, mystery, and metals. Alchemy is an early form of science that was a forerunner of many of the subjects that you can study in college today, such as chemistry (the study of the substances that compose matter), metallurgy (the study of metals), and pharmaceuticals (the science of medicinal drugs). Alchemy is famously associated with the quest to prolong life and to transform base metals into precious ones, such as changing tin into silver, or transforming lead into gold. Alchemy is also associated with problem-solving and with finding "solutions" in general. In addition to the magical elixir that could transmute base metals into precious ones, alchemists also sought to create a substance called an alkahest. This is a universal solvent that could solve problems and dissolve other substances.[2]

In turn, a mirror is a surface that can reflect something desirable that you want to model (or mirror) for yourself, *or* something undesirable that you want to clear out or avoid. Alchemy too is associated with manifesting something that you want, or getting rid of something that you don't want. Alchemy and reflection are like two sides of the same silver coin.

Silver can be used as a color of great alchemy because it is a wonderful transmuter of all kinds of energies. Silver has strong antimicrobial properties, which means that it can transmute different illnesses in the physical body, whether they are viral or bacterial. Silver can help to change the frequency of something that is low and dense and bring it into a bright shiny clarity.

When you gaze into a looking glass, silver can help you to see what the mirrors of your body are reflecting, and what your thoughts and feelings are showing you. Silver can also help you to wash the mirrors clean so that you can see a new reflection and find new ways to sparkle. When you do the hard work of self-reflection and introspection—when you look deeply into your own mind and heart, and you make important changes in your perspective and your behavior—it is like you are scrubbing out the inside of a pot so that the silver can shine through.

Sometimes when we look at ourselves in the mirror, we see something that we think has little to no value. We may have lost our sense of value, our sense of beauty, and our sense of connection to what is cherished. Sometimes we seek this value in outside objects. But outside objects only ever reflect what is already inside of us. These objects are like mirrors because they reflect how we feel about ourselves and how we hold ourselves in the world. The integrity, the grace, and the compassion we hold ourselves in will always reflect outside of us, in the outer world.

In so many ways, the inner and the outer are mirror images of one another.

The words "mirror", "miracle", and "admire" all share a common root, which means to look at, to wonder at, and to smile.[3] When you trust your own wisdom and your own perceptions, you value yourself in a new way. Silver can be like a mirror that holds these reflections as you look at yourself in a new way, and you wonder, and you admire—and you smile.

Exercises for Experiential Learning, Visualization, and Reflection

- Sometimes in life, fragments of the everyday world can appear to be radiant. In your own life, can you identify an apparently ordinary object that holds tremendous value and significance for you? What is the object, and why does it matter so deeply? How does looking at a seemingly ordinary object in such an expansive way transform your own perspective?

- Consider bringing the object to class so that students can share their stories and reflect collectively on their expanded conceptions of presence and value.

- To show care for yourself, you can undertake a mirror exercise by constructing a self-portrait, either in words or images, or both. As you do this, you can ask yourself: What do you value in yourself, and why? Do you recognize special inner qualities reflected in your own physical features? In your own expressions? In your own eyes? In your own smile? Why are these qualities so valuable? How does this distinctive combination of the inner and the outer uniquely make you, you?

Notes

 1 Fancy Pants Reference Point: Since early 2009, it has been my privilege to serve as a literary Artist In Residence in the Department of Palliative, Rehabilitation, and Integrative Medicine at the University of Texas M.D. Anderson Cancer Center. Since early 2021, I have also been serving as a Literary Artist at the Hospital of the University of Pennsylvania. My work is sponsored by COLLAGE: The Art for Cancer Network, a non-profit organization conceived and founded by Dr. Jennifer Wheler. COLLAGE is dedicated to providing innovative art programs for people living with cancer. For information on this nonprofit organization, see https://collageforcancer.org.

 2 See the entry on "alchemy" in the *OED*: https://www-oed-com.ezproxy .rice.edu/viewdictionaryentry/Entry/4691.

3 Fancy Pants Reference Point: The common root comes from the Latin word *mirari*, which expresses a sense of wonder. See the entries on "mirror", "miracle", and "admire" in *Webster's Seventh New Collegiate Dictionary* (Springfield, MA: G. & C. Merriam, 1969), pp. 540, 12.

Reference list

Simpson, J. A., and E. S. C. Weiner, eds. *The Oxford English Dictionary*. 2nd ed. Oxford: Clarendon Press, 1989.

Webster's Seventh New Collegiate Dictionary. Springfield, MA: G. & C. Merriam, 1969.

Chapter 9: The School of Gold

Reimagining Values, Treasures, and Transitions

Much like silver, gold is a color of treasure and transition on the physical, emotional, and spiritual levels at once. When you hear the word "gold", so many images come to mind: money, jewelry, a grandmother's ring. Like silver, gold is a natural element found in the Earth. It is also a strong bridge between the subtle and the physical worlds. Gold is as solid as the coin in your pocket, and as ethereal as the gentle light of dawn.

When I was little, I saw that my aunts, my mother, and both of my grandmothers wore golden wedding rings on the third finger of their left hand. One of my grandmothers also had a round gold watch that she wore on a chain around her

DOI: 10.4324/9781032613697-10

neck. The watch was made of rose gold, so it was a warm pinkish-gold with a delicate floral design etched on its surface.[1] The watch had a notch at the top and, if you pressed in carefully, the metal case popped open and you could see the time.

My grandmother had inherited this watch from her mother, my great-grandmother. My great-grandmother was born in Italy, and she passed away many decades before I was born, so I never got to meet her. Many years after my own grandmother passed away, my father gave the watch to me. Like my grandmother, I wear the watch on very special occasions. But unlike my grandmother, I don't use the watch to tell time. Instead, I wear the watch around my neck like a locket. A locket is a little container that holds precious things. For me, the rose gold locket holds cherished memories and connections to the grandmother I knew and loved so well, and to the great-grandmother whom I never got to meet.

Gold is often used in jewelry because this precious metal is soft enough to be molded and sculpted into many beautiful forms. Gold is a source of great value and beauty on many levels at once. Sometimes gold thread is used in rich fabrics and textiles, and sometimes a very thin layer of melted gold, called gold leaf, is applied to the surfaces of wood or metal for ornamentation.

Gold is also associated with the value of money. Historically, the American economy was based on the gold standard, which means that the value of the nation's currency (such as the dollar) was guaranteed by a certain amount of gold.[2] Yet the term "gold standard" refers to much more than the value of money. A gold standard is a measure of excellence. It is a way of saying that something is of the very highest quality, and it is the very best of its kind. Sometimes people who are extremely kind and generous are described as having hearts of gold. These people may appear very ordinary on the outside, but they have many beautiful and valuable qualities on the inside.

Sometimes in life, ordinary things can be very precious. Treasured objects can hold special meaning and value because they are associated with a particular person or memory, just as my grandmother's rose gold watch is special to me. Whenever I wear it, I feel safe and protected. I feel like my grandmother and my great-grandmother are with me, even though they are no longer here. Like many family heirlooms and old photographs, my grandmother's locket serves as a tangible link between generations, and as a way to feel people's subtle presences. Perhaps you have such a treasure of your own?

Gold is a color of change and exchange. Gold can take the form of something solid—like a piece of jewelry—or something fluid, like the fluctuating value of currency, or shifting patterns of sunlight. Gold is a bridge between the world that you can see with your physical eyes and the one that you cannot. The rose gold locket is such a bridge between worlds. The locket provides a connection between those who are here now, and those who are no longer here.

One day while I was working at the hospital, a woman told me how much she treasured her childhood memories of her grandparents, and especially, of her great-grandmother. She also told me how much she valued her connections to her ancestors in general—to all of the family members who came before her. Even though she was going through an extremely difficult illness, the woman also felt that

There's a Light There, As Well

My spirituality connects me to my ancestors,
To my grandparents and to my great-grandmother.
I had my grandparents growing up,
And I was super close to my great-grandmother.

Since they've passed away
I have felt their presences,
And I believe they are here with us.

This makes me feel guarded and protected,
And I know that everything is going to be okay.

My grandparents are always there for me,
Whenever I need them.
I feel like, even though I'm going through a hard time,
There's a light there, as well.

Another elderly man told me about the special connection he has with his father:

We Have a Certain Bond

I lost my dad a few months ago.
He was my best friend.
My father always told me stories of how he grew up,
And all the hardships he had to overcome.
He never stopped.

He never quit.
He never gave up,
And he learned his craft.

We would always talk.
You've got to have guidance in your life.
It calms you and it helps you,
And then you can go forward.

After my dad passed,
I would sometimes see him in my dreams.
He looked the same,
Except that he looked like he was surrounded by gold.

My dad has a strong personality,
And he has a strong voice.
It's a voice you can't forget.
I can still hear him.
We have a certain bond.

Life is filled with such transitions. A transition is a change, and it can be like a kind of doorway. During times of transition, it is important for people to feel safe and accompanied. When you think of life transitions, you can always think of the soft golden light that appears around the edges of a door that might otherwise seem to be closed.

Another way to think about transitions is to picture the beautiful golden light of dawn that comes after a dark night—a light that we welcome so eagerly in the morning. When we sit in the bright golden light, we sit in a shield of sunlight, and we can feel a sense of calm and ease. We feel a sense of certainty that everything is happening exactly the way that it is supposed to be happening. There is an overall sense of rightness to it all, like the magnificent golden light that moves so easily across the sky.

Gold is the color of treasures and transitions. It is soft and bright and very protective. It is like my great-grandmother's locket, which is the gold that I keep close to my heart.

Exercises for Experiential Learning, Visualization, and Reflection

- As a way to explore the relationships between tangible and symbolic systems of value, bring a metal coin or a paper one-dollar bill to class. Place the items on your desktop and, in your journal, reflect on how these objects are at once distinctly special *and* extremely common and ordinary. Then, imagine how it would feel to tear up the paper bill or throw the coin in the trash can. (Don't actually discard the money; just see and feel yourself doing this, in your mind's eye.) What does this exercise teach you about the ways in which abstract conceptions of value become paired with concrete objects and their material reference points? Why is this imaginative exercise so powerful?

- This exercise also demonstrates the concept of paradox, because two seemingly opposite conditions are present at the same time (in this case, the ordinary and the special). Can you think of other examples of paradox? What are they, and what is distinctive about them?

- Do you have a family heirloom, such as a treasured photograph or a piece of jewelry, that connects you to your ancestors? How does this material object serve as a link between the abstract and the concrete domains? How does this material object serve as a link between yourself, who is present, and those who are no longer present? Why do you value these connections in your life?

- How is the photograph or the heirloom an example of a paradox, as it embodies a simultaneous state of presence and absence, of the material and the subtle, the common and the special? What does sentimental value have in common with material value, and how are they different? Why is it powerful to be able to apprehend such multiple perspectives at once?

- Can you think of someone in your life who has a heart of gold, who exemplifies many beautiful and valuable qualities on the inside? Who is this individual, and why do you admire them and value their presence? Have you ever told this person that you recognize their heart of gold, and that you are grateful for their presence in your life?

- Go outside with your journal, sit under a tree, and pay careful attention to how the bright golden sunlight moves fluidly across the sky and through the tree leaves. Can you feel a sense of ease and rightness as you carefully observe the gentle motions of the ever-shifting sunlight? Why is it important to practice being present and consciously aware as change occurs? Record your thoughts and observations in your journal.

Notes

1 Fancy Pants Reference Point: Gold can come in many different colors. Sometimes gold is mixed with small amounts of other elements, such as zinc or copper. These mixtures are called alloys. The amount of the metal in the mixture determines the purity, and thus, the number of carats of the gold. Pure gold is 24 carats. When yellow gold is mixed with palladium or nickel, it produces white gold. When yellow gold is mixed

with copper, it produces rose gold. And when yellow gold is mixed with silver and copper, it produces green gold. For a technical discussion of the alloy composition of gold, see the entry on "Gold and Gold Alloys" in *Total Materia* (November 2009): https://www.totalmateria.com/page .aspx?ID=CheckArticle&site=ktn&NM=230.

2 Fancy Pants Reference Point: The United States was on the gold standard until 1971. Today, the U.S. dollar and other global currencies such as the Euro are called fiat-money because they are issued by the governments that back them. Even though the United States is no longer on the gold standard, vast stockpiles of gold are part of the nation's wealth. The United States's gold reserves are kept in fortified vaults operated by the Department of the Treasury. The best known of these is Fort Knox, which is the United States Bullion Depository located next to the army post of Fort Knox, Kentucky. For more information on the United States Bullion Depository, see: https://www.usmint.gov/about/mint-tours-facilities/fort-knox. For the entries on "gold standard" and "fiat-money" in the *OED*, see: https://www-oed-com.ezproxy.rice.edu/viewdictionary-entry/Entry/60986342 and https://www-oed-com.ezproxy.rice.edu/view/Entry/69729?redirectedFrom=fiat+money#eid4394015.

Reference list

"Gold and Gold Alloys." *Total Materia,* November 2009. https://www .totalmateria.com/page.aspx?ID=CheckArticle&site=ktn&NM=230.

Simpson, J. A., and E. S. C. Weiner, eds. *The Oxford English Dictionary*. 2nd ed. Oxford: Clarendon Press, 1989.

Chapter 10: The School of Pink

Compassion, Care, Generosity, and the Superpower of a Loving Heart

Pink evokes a purity of heart. This color is associated with unconditional love, which is a love that is given freely, without limitations. When you think of the color pink, you can think of the power of compassion. Compassion is the emotion you feel when you notice that someone is in distress, and you feel moved to help or support that person. Compassion is the gentle art of being present, combined with the great strength of bearing something difficult together. This is like giving someone a gift straight from the heart.

DOI: 10.4324/9781032613697-11

At different times in our life, we all need compassion. When I was in the third grade, my little sister had to have her tonsils out. She is my only sister, and I was extremely concerned about the entire situation. On the day she went to the hospital, I went to school as usual. I already knew that when I came home later that afternoon, my mother would not be there, because she would be staying overnight at the hospital with my sister. What I did *not* expect to find was a box on the kitchen table containing a gift for me. The card read, "Marcia, I know you are worried and that your mother can't be with you. Maybe you can accept me as a substitute?" Inside the box was a soft white lamb with a little golden bell around its neck. My mother understood how upset I was about my sister, and she generously left this present to comfort me. Because my mother saw how concerned I was about my sister, she gave me a present to relieve my own distress. In the middle of a difficult experience, my mother's generosity and compassion created something beautiful that I cherish to this day.

To be compassionate is to be sympathetic to another person, especially when you see that they are in pain or suffering. Compassion always involves a heightened sense of awareness and kindness. Sometimes when people are in pain, what they need the most is someone to talk to. When they talk to you, you are practicing a powerful skill called compassionate listening.

One afternoon while I was working at the hospital, I met a woman who was extremely sick, and whose beautiful clear eyes were filled with a soft light. When I asked the woman about the imagery that was important to her, she told me how much she appreciated all that her children did to help her. She used the gift of our time together to create a gift for her own children, a narrative artwork that she dedicated to them. Just as the woman's story is filled with unconditional love, her words show how there are no such things as small things. The woman lovingly told me that her children are

The Biggest Help That I Have

I would like to give something to my kids,
To make them happy and smiling.
My kids always try to help out, and to keep a good attitude.
It's incredible to see how all of them have stepped up.
My teenage daughter is an especially big help.
I don't know what I'd do without her.
She does everything.

She does all the little things I need,
And she keeps such a good attitude.
She's the biggest help that I have.

She and my sons stay close to me the whole time.
They do it all on their own,
And they're so awesome about it.
They are my heart.

Because the woman's children gave her so much help during her time of need, all of the ordinary little things that they did were *not* small things. These gestures were big things, and everything mattered very deeply. The woman wanted her children to know that she appreciated all that they did for her, and that she loved them with her whole heart.

Recently I was thinking about children and the beauty of compassion while I was walking in the Japanese Garden at Hermann Park. At one point I found myself standing under a grove of flowering crape myrtle trees. The blossoms were beautiful shades of soft raspberry and rose pink. The trees were planted by a little wooden footbridge, and under the bridge was a small waterfall. Most of the blossoms were still on the trees, but some had already fallen, and they were floating gently on the water. This image made me think of compassion and care, as you will see at the end of this chapter.

As I stood on the little wooden footbridge, a group of first graders and their teacher approached from the opposite side of the park. The children crossed the bridge two by two, each holding hands with a partner. When they saw the blossoms floating on the water, all the boys and girls stopped to look. Some looked longer and more deeply than others, but every child stopped, and they all saw the beauty.

There are so many stories that I could tell you about children and the beauty of compassion, but I'll share just one more. One day I met a woman who was an elementary school teacher. Her close friend was also a teacher in the same school. I asked the woman what drew her and her friend to the important work of teaching. The hallmark of the woman's story is the color pink, with its intertwined qualities of compassion, softness, and strength. This tender yet powerful story may be especially meaningful for those of you who are drawn to the field of education. As the woman told me:

They Capture Your Heart

My friend and I work in the same school,
At the Elementary School level.
I would see my friend in the hallways,
Between classes.
Her eyes were always so bright.
You could always tell
She was so happy to be there.

Her message to the kids was always:
"Anyone who has a 'why' has a 'how'".

The children are so true.
They capture your heart,
And you never want to let them go.

Children will naturally flock to someone who radiates this kind of compassion, kindness, and reassurance. Perhaps you are one of those people? You may be very good at radiating kindness and reassurance to others. This muscle may be very strong, especially when you are doing it for someone else. You may even be like a bodybuilder in that department, like someone who can lift heavy weights. When you practice compassion toward yourself, it may be a bit more challenging. As you practice this skill, you may think that you are building a new muscle, but you are not. You are just learning how to use the muscles that you already have differently.

Pink is like a heart-to-heart transmission that you can give to yourself or to another. When you feel compassion towards someone, it is like you are radiating pink in their direction. It is like you are offering the person a rose plucked from a shrub in your own backyard.

Pink is one of the most powerful energies of the whole universe. To feel compassion for another can melt a hard heart.

Because pink blends red and white, this color combines great vitality and passion with great purity and delicacy. Because pink is composed partly of white, it is a color that contains *all* of the colors. This is why pink can go anywhere. This is why compassion can go into the hardest and darkest places. This is why pink is a superpower. It is the total power of your loving heart.

Exercises for Experiential Learning, Visualization, and Reflection

• Imagine that you are standing on the little wooden footbridge in the Japanese garden. Your feet are on firm ground, even as you look down and see the water running swiftly over the rocks beneath you. The water can be like a difficult life situation unfolding around you or another person. When you encounter someone who is having a hard time, you can imagine yourself standing on the bridge with that person while you both gaze downward into the running water. As you offer your compassion to the person, you can think of your kindness and caring as being like the pink blossoms that float so softly on the turbulent surface of the water rushing beneath your feet.

- Do you know someone who is in pain or in need? This could be an elderly person or someone who has experienced a loss, an illness, or an injury. If you were in their situation, would you appreciate someone reaching out to you with great gentleness and delicacy? How would you do this? What would such a soft and caring gesture look like? What words would you use, and how would you feel? How can such small gestures of kindness be so powerful? How might your very presence be a gift to someone else?

- Animals can help open the door to compassion as they open people's hearts. Sometimes it is much easier to feel at ease towards a cat or a dog than towards a mother or father or sibling—or even, towards yourself. If it is difficult for you to have compassion for yourself, you can always imagine yourself sitting with a special animal. This can be any kind of animal—a dog, a cat, a rabbit, a horse, a bird, a turtle, a squirrel—it can be any creature. If you love cats, for example, you can always see yourself sitting with a beautiful cat in your lap, purring and purring and purring. The cat is radiating unconditional acceptance and unconditional love for you and for whatever is going on with you. You can see this very clearly in your mind's eye, and you can know that, even if you can't always connect to yourself, you can *always* connect to this beautiful animal.

- There are many ways to offer yourself care and compassion. You can always tell yourself, "I am so sad today. I am going to do something nice for myself today". Then you can imagine giving yourself a gift. You can picture a beautiful box wrapped in bright pink paper with a gold ribbon around it. See yourself holding the box in your left hand—the hand closest to your heart—and placing it into your right. As you give yourself the gift, you can feel a strong sense of self-love as your heart expands even further.

Chapter 11: The School of Black and White

Bending Light, Flicking the Switch, and Seeing Multiple Perspectives at Once

Now that we are approaching the end of this book, it may interest you to know that scholars and scientists do not share a single or unified understanding of the subject of color. Can you believe it?! It's true. Just as artists adopt many different approaches to the use of color in their paintings and sculptures, scientists and researchers hold many different opinions regarding exactly what color is, where color is, and even whether color is an object or a subject (or both).[1] Color is mysterious and intriguing. And no matter how much we know, there will still always be so much more to know.

You could explore all of the colors for a thousand years and still never know all of their secrets, all of their mysteries, all of their magic, or the depths of their powers. There would still always be more. No two colors exemplify this sense of the "always more" more than black and white. While black and white often appear as opposites, these colors can be approached as powerful complements.

In both art and in science, white is all color with light, and black is all color without light.[2] While white is very bright and black is very dark, both colors contain all the visible wavelengths of light. This means that they are the colors that contain *all* of the colors.

While black and white are everywhere, all around us, sometimes they can be difficult to see. Just as the structure of this book is prismatic, one way to study color is to look through a prism. A prism is a piece of transparent glass whose sides have been cut at different angles to form sharp facets. When white light passes through the angled sides of a prism, the individual colors become visible.

During the 1660s, the English mathematician, astronomer, and physicist Sir Isaac Newton (1643–1727) experimented with passing sunlight through prisms. As he

DOI: 10.4324/9781032613697-12

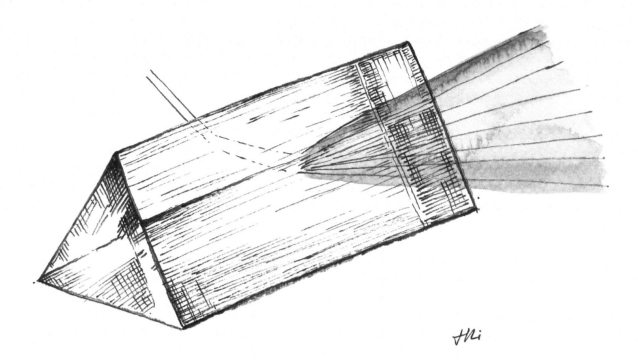

did so, Newton discovered that white light contains the seven primary colors of the spectrum: red, orange, yellow, green, blue, indigo, and violet (ROYGBIV, for short). Newton documented his findings in his treatise on *Opticks* (1704), which is an extremely important book in the history of science. As the experiments showed, as light passes through a prism, it changes direction, and it bends. The individual colors then become separated because each color bends at a different angle. When the bent light waves are seen through a prism, they form the arcing shape of a rainbow.[3]

While all of the spectral colors are always present in white light, you can't see them unless you have a tool such as a prism. You can think of black in a similar way. Just as black holds all of the colors, you can't see them without the aid of light.

Imagine that you are standing in a completely dark room. The room may be filled with many colorful objects, but you can't see them unless you turn on a light switch. When you flick the switch, the darkness doesn't disappear. It just recedes and integrates with the light. You are still standing in exactly the same room, with exactly the same objects, whether the lights are on or off. You just see the same room very differently.

In your mind, imagine that you are standing in such a completely dark room. Then imagine flicking the light switch on—and then, off—and then on again—and watching the world appear—and disappear—and appear again, in a new light.

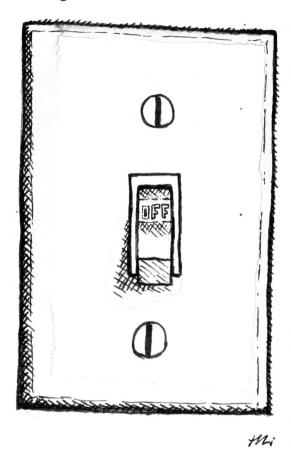

Black and white are often seen as opposites, but in many ways, they are complements. Throughout history, the color white has been used to show how important people carry their power. White light often appears like a halo around the bodies of powerful individuals to emphasize qualities that would otherwise remain invisible, such as inner wisdom, kindness, and compassion.

The color black is also extremely powerful. Black is associated with the magic of the unknown. This is the color of those who are not afraid of the dark. These individuals can go into the dark and it does not affect them, no matter what is happening there, and no matter what they can or cannot see.

Black and white are complements. When people see the world only in terms of black or white, they tend to hold rigid mindsets. They tend to think, "It is all this, or it is all that". Black and white are the places where opposites meet. Just as these colors are found at the extreme ends of the spectrum, you can think of them as the bookends that hold the middle together.

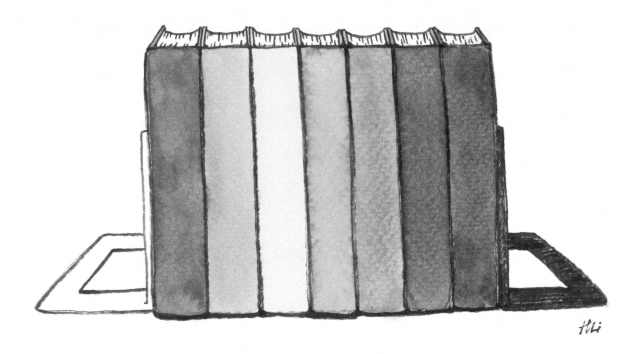

When you no longer see the world in terms of "black and white", then you see with both your inner and your outer eyes. You see how black and white complete one another, and how together, they bring a sense of wholeness. Thinking deeply about black and white can help you to see multiple, diverse—and sometimes, competing—perspectives, all at once. This is a special kind of vision. It is like looking at life through the many facets of a crystal prism all at once and seeing a coherent picture emerge. Such composite vision can allow for great nuance and complexity. Much like black and white, this special type of prismatic vision has the potential to hold everything. And that is why—like black and white—it is a tool for creating worlds.

Exercises for Experiential Learning, Visualization, and Reflection

- Obtain a crystal prism and note the relationships between clear white light and the colorful tonal spectrum that emerges as sunlight passes through the facets of the glass. Why is it valuable to see the unseen depths, perspectives, and qualities that can reside within a seemingly unified object? Why is it important to remember that multiplicity can exist within unity?
- If you live in a climate where there is snow, go outside and look closely at the sunlight shining on newly fallen snow. At first, you may think it is only white. But if you look more closely, you will see that the snow is every color. Make notes in your journal about the colors that you observe within the

whiteness of the snow, and how the air "feels white" when snowflakes fall from the sky.

- Identify a complex issue in which multiple perspectives are simultaneously valid. Formulate responses to account for these multiple points of view. What can you learn by shifting positions and arguing multiple sides of a question?
- Write an original story with a simple plot line. Then, tell exactly the same narrative from three or four different points of view. How are the various stories both similar *and* different? How can multiple—even, seemingly contradictory—viewpoints all be possible at the same time?
- Why is it powerful to have such an expansive perspective of life that extends beyond the rigid boundaries of "black and white"?

Notes

1 Fancy Pants Reference Point: The scholar David Scott Kastan puts the matter aptly when he observes that "Chemists tend to locate [color] in the microphysical properties of colored objects; physicists in the specific frequencies of electromagnetic energy that those objects reflect; physiologists in the photoreceptors of the eye that detect this energy; and neurobiologists in the neural processing of this information by the brain. Their disagreement, or more accurately, the mismatch of their inquiry, seems to suggest that color inhabits some indistinct borderland between the objective and the subjective, the phenomenal and the psychological". See David Scott Kastan, *On Color* (New Haven: Yale University Press, 2018), p. 2. This volume provides a thoughtful account of the history of spectral colors and their various lexical, artistic, historical, cultural, and literary usages.

2 Fancy Pants Reference Point: As the *OED* notes: "From a scientific perspective, the quality of being white is due to the equal reflection or emission of all wavelengths of the visible spectrum of light; white objects therefore lack any distinctive hue". In turn, "From a scientific perspective, the quality of being black is due to the absence or absorption of all the wavelengths of light occurring in the visible spectrum". See the entries on "white" and "black" in the *OED*: https://www-oed -com.ezproxy.rice.edu/viewdictionaryentry/Entry/228566 and https:// www-oed-com.ezproxy.rice.edu/viewdictionaryentry/Entry/19670.

 3   See the entry on "prism" in the *OED*: https://www-oed-com.ezproxy.rice .edu/view/Entry/151542?redirectedFrom=prism#eid.

Reference list

Kastan, David Scott. *On Color.* New Haven: Yale University Press, 2018.

Simpson, J. A., and E. S. C. Weiner, eds. *The Oxford English Dictionary.* 2nd ed. Oxford: Clarendon Press, 1989.

Chapter 12: Putting the Pieces Together to Build a House Made Out of Color

Because black and white are the colors that hold all of the colors, they are the basic tools of creation and worldbuilding. Black and white are like the ink and the paper. They are the foundational elements that form the structures of the books that you read and the buildings that you live in. And, both books and buildings are composed of many different stories.

Black and white are like the outlines of a coloring book whose blank pages are just waiting to be filled in. All of the colors are tools of worldbuilding, and they all relate to one another in distinct and creative ways. You could spend entire lifetimes exploring these relationships…

DOI: 10.4324/9781032613697-13

But for now, let's practice creating something specific. Because black and white contain everything, they can be used to build practically anything, including a house made out of color. If you were to construct such a house, you might begin by thinking about the materials that form the building's foundation and its facade. Red bricks would give your house great strength and stability. When you walk through the back door—which is the door that everybody goes to except those who are strangers, who always go to the front door—you might find yourself standing in a kitchen. You can see the inviting warmth of a red brick fireplace. You notice that food is being prepared so creatively in the kitchen, and you feel a warm orange glow rising in your belly. When you step to the side of the kitchen, you might find yourself standing in a bright sunroom that is filled with peaceful yellow light and flourishing green plants. You can look out the big windows and see vibrant green trees and shrubs, and a fragrant pink rosebush flowering in the backyard. You can also look up and see the vast blue sky over your head. When twilight comes, you can flick on the light switch and see the dark room fill up with light. Then you can walk upstairs to a bedroom where shimmering indigo light shines through several large glass windows. Before entering the dreamtime, you can take a book off the shelf and read about the kings and queens of old who changed the world as they sat on their thrones in their splendid violet robes. Before you turn off the light, you might look at your own reflection in a silver mirror and admire what you see. When the room is completely dark, you may notice the bright golden light around the edges of a door that is almost closed. And, when you wake up in the morning, you can see the soft golden light streaming in through the same large glass windows.

Everything comes through these open doors and through these open windows.

Now, look out the window:

The Spark Begins

Imagine that you are looking up at the clouds,
At giant high buildings and towers of clouds,
All white tinged with pink.
If you placed your hands with your palms together,
One palm would be the dominant hand.
This is the hand of creation.
The other is the hand of recognition.
Putting your hands palms together
In a gesture of offering,
You place them into the clouds.
You then open up the pink from the white,
And you allow the silver and the gold to come through.
And then, the spark begins.
And lo and behold,
There is life.

Now, what if I told you that you could explore the color blue for a thousand years?...

Exercises for Experiential Learning, Visualization, and Reflection

- If you were to build a house made out of color, what would it look like? How would the different parts relate to the whole?
- How does it feel to occupy this house, and what is the view outside the windows?
- How does your house made of color reflect the relations between your own inner and outer worlds?
- What makes this house uniquely your own?

(There Is No) Conclusion

The Magic of Your Favorite Colors: Chromatics, Gratitude, Illumination

Many people have a favorite color, and some people have more than one. Sometimes people have a favorite color throughout their entire lifetime, and sometimes a person's favorite color changes over time. Do you have a favorite color? It may be that more than one color comes up. That's fine. Just listen carefully and pay close attention to whatever arises.

Here is the magical part: Once you identified your favorite color, you instantly began to turn that color into your own energy field. You did this without even thinking because you got excited about that color. This is how you know that you have a natural flair for that color.

DOI: 10.4324/9781032613697-14

At a very basic level, the universe is made of the frequencies of light and sound. A word that describes both light and sound is "chromatic". Chromatic means relating to color.[1] When you feel a color in your mind, you instantly get an idea of the subtle energy that color is holding. You can always ask yourself: "What lies beyond the word 'red'? What resonates with it, and what does not? What runs away from red, and what runs towards it?"

When an object displays multiple colors, it is called polychromatic. This word literally means multicolored. If you want to imagine a polychromatic object, you can think of a crazy quilt—a quilt in which bright colors and fabrics are placed together to form an irregular patchwork of colorful patterns. If you want to get really imaginative, in your mind's eye you can picture a small table harp. When the harp is strummed, rainbows of sound come out.

Just as material objects can be polychromatic, complex emotions can also be made of many different colors. Gratitude is a wonderful example of this. You may find yourself asking: "What color is gratitude? Is gratitude a particular color, or can it be all the colors?" Gratitude can be a combination of all the colors, based on where this emotion is coming from, and what is added to it. Sometimes we are grateful that something didn't happen to us. Sometimes we are grateful for something we have. Sometimes we are grateful that we are moving forward. Sometimes we are grateful that we are left behind. Sometimes we are grateful that we are simply in love. Sometimes we are in love with a person, or an animal, or an item, or a planet, or a tree, or a star.

The color of gratitude all depends on where the thankfulness is falling.

You can envision pure gratitude as an extremely pale, buttery yellow, almost like a rich creamy ivory. This is a warm foundational color and, like a blank canvas, many colors can be added to it over time. Because you will be grateful for so many different things throughout your lifetime, you can always weave different colors into the pale ivory light at different moments in your life.

One day I met a woman who was extremely grateful for the time she got to spend on a ranch while growing up as a child. The woman's imagery is filled with the strong yet delicate colors of this rich outdoor world, and its distinctive shades of sage and alfalfa green, cotton candy red, and sky blue:

Sage and Sky

When I was growing up, one of my uncles had a ranch.
The ranch had horses, sheep, and cattle.
At the ranch, there was always the smell of alfalfa.
It's the greatest smell in the world.
It's fresh, and it is so delightful that,
Now I put a little plate of alfalfa in my house.
It's in my dining room,
On the sideboard,
Right next to the sage.
The sage is so relaxing.
It's healing, and it's protective.
The sage is a light grayish-green color,
And it smells really good.

At the ranch, outside at night,
The sky looked like a soft, cotton candy red.
This made me feel warm.
By day, there was the nice blue sky,
With the sun shining.

These are all open spaces,
Where all you can see is sky,
And it feels like freedom.

Because gratitude has the capacity to hold and reflect so much energy, you can always think of gratitude as being like the first rays of sun in the eastern sky. This is a special kind of illumination. This type of light can create a strong, conscious connection between your inner and your outer worlds.

One day I met a man who loved his home very deeply. When I asked him why this place was so special, he told me how, where he lives,

The Sky Holds Everything

We have a ranch by the mountains.
There is a little white house and a red barn.
The sky is amazing.

From our back door,
We can see the sunsets forever.
If it's clear outside,
The sky is just like dripping color.

And then, there's the last ray of sunlight,
That just catches you.
It's breathtaking.
You cannot put a price on that.
I think about the sky,
Because the sky is so big.
Sometimes life is hard,
But it is beautiful, too.
The sky holds everything.

Just as the man said, the sky can hold all of the colors. The sky is always shifting, and it is always radiant. The sky is big enough to hold everything. And for this sense of spaciousness, he was so grateful.

When you approach the world this way, you begin to see with both your outer and your inner eyes.

This book joins the two worlds together—the outer world that you can see with your physical eyes, and the inner world that you can feel in your mind and heart. Color is a powerful bridge between the outer and the inner worlds, between the visible and the invisible domains.

Some people might call this obvious.

Others might call it magic…

Exercises for Experiential Learning, Visualization, and Reflection

- What are your favorite colors, and why do these hues resonate so deeply for you? Has your favorite color changed as you have read this book?
- How can colors serve as powerful bridges between the inner and the outer domains—between the subtle realms of thought and emotion, and the physical world that we experience with our senses? How does this unfold in ways that are at once readily familiar *and* absolutely extraordinary?
- What are you especially grateful for, and why? Which tonal qualities do you see reflected in your own gratitude?

- As a group, students can share their special objects or stories of gratitude. The class can conclude with an overall reflection on: Why is gratitude so powerful? What are we all grateful for together, and why?

Note

 1 Fancy Pants Reference Point: If you were to map the wavelengths and the frequencies of all of the colors that you can see with your eyes, you would have what is called the chromatic scale of the visible spectrum. If you were to apply this concept to sound, then the chromatic scale would refer to the twelve-tone scale of the pitches of tonal music. See the entry on "chromatic" in the *OED*: https://www-oed-com.ezproxy.rice .edu/view/Entry/32504?redirectedFrom=chromatic+scale#eid9373495. Notably, in his chromatic experiments, Sir Isaac Newton also correlated color values with corresponding musical notations.

Reference list

Simpson, J. A., and E. S. C. Weiner, eds. *The Oxford English Dictionary*. 2nd ed. Oxford: Clarendon Press, 1989.

P.S. Guess What I Just Told Your Teacher?

Notice how the letters "P.S." sound a lot like a secret, like, "Psssss...I've got something to tell you". P.S. is actually an abbreviation for "postscript", which means writing that comes after the main body of a text, such as a letter, or in this case, a book. And yes, I am going to let you in on a little secret. Psssss...

You may already know that I wrote a companion guide to *The Colors of Life*. This book is written for teachers, parents, counselors, librarians, and school leaders, and it is entitled *Approaching SEL Through Emotion and Color With Advanced Learners: A Companion to The Colors of Life*. Much like the book that you are holding in your hands, the companion guide begins with an invitation. The invitation is followed by a set of vivid keywords and sentences inviting teachers to think about color in very creative ways so that they can contemplate what it would be like to teach color and emotion in their own classrooms.

You may well be asking, "Why did I do this?" Excellent question. Please remember that I too am a teacher. As I was writing *The Colors of Life*, I realized that we were facing a kind of riddle, namely: As students read *The Colors of Life* and experience the colors and emotions for themselves, then they (i.e. *all of you*) will know far more about these important subjects than your own teachers, because you will have experienced these subjects directly and not just read about them intellectually, in a book. This will create a situation where the students will have a stronger understanding of the subjects being taught than the people who are supposed to be guiding them through this exploration.

All of this posed an interesting challenge, namely: How does the teacher learn? Clearly, something (fun) had to be done. So, I developed the list of keywords and accompanying images. In case you're wondering, here they are:

The keyword for the color red is root. You can always think of tree roots going deep into the soil, or a rich root vegetable coming up from the earth. Red is an invitation to take a breath and sink deeply into your body. Red invites you to take a moment to feel a little more grounded, to anchor in more deeply, and

DOI: 10.4324/9781032613697-15

to feel the awareness of your body flowing down from your mind into your own roots.

Orange is like the warm glow of a welcoming kitchen. Orange is a bit of a loving hug, a warm embrace that feels like a sleeping kitten—soft, supple, and trusting. Orange is like a warm kitchen with cookies baking in the oven. As soon as you walk through the door on a cold day, you immediately receive a warm hug.

The keyword for yellow is center. Yellow is like an inner mirror of self-awareness and self-reflection. Deep in the pit of your stomach, in your own gut, you know how you truly feel about things, and you constantly reflect these feelings back to yourself. Yellow is the inner sense of self-awareness that sits at your very center. Yellow reflects how you really feel, and not what the external world projects onto you or tells you about what you want and how you should be feeling. Yellow is like a mirror that reflects what is going on deep inside yourself, at your very center.

Green inspires a strong sense of regeneration, like the new leaves of spring that bring fresh waves of life and energy throughout the entire landscape. Green brings fresh energy throughout an entire system. It is like sloughing off a heavy old winter coat on a warm day so that you can move lightly and easily through the world. Green inspires a welcome sense of growth and renewal, both in the natural world and in you.

The keywords for blue are open, expansive, receptive, and vulnerable. Blue is like the western sky just after sunset, a time of day when the fading rays of sunlight illuminate the blue sky in depth. This is a time of day when you begin to move more freely. This usually happens just after sunset, when the outpouring of the day's activities slows down. Everyone begins to unwind and calm down, and they become more communicative. Maybe they're all sitting and having a meal together. Or, maybe they're just sitting in the same room together, asking each other, "How was your day?" The words begin to flow more easily, more fluidly, and more truthfully, without all the hurries of the day. In that resting time there is an openness, and a receptivity, and a sense of vulnerability. Everyone winds down naturally, in the softness of the blue.

Indigo reflects a willingness to change. Indigo can venture deep into the darkest places and see what is truly there. This color can instantly cut through illusions to see the world in a new light. Indigo loves to change, which is why this hue sometimes appears in a shade of purple, and sometimes in a shade of blue. Indigo moves and shimmers and goes gracefully from place to place, always willing to see everything without any illusions, and always willing to be true to oneself. Indigo is a visionary, always willing to see the world anew.

Violet is a supreme color; it is the color of kings and queens. Violet is the great power that couples a sense of sovereignty with a sense of freedom. From the vulnerability of blue, and the willingness to change of indigo, violet is the place where real transformation arises. This is where things get really interesting. Change becomes the new reality, and change is always moving toward greater freedom. Like the blue-violet light at the center of a flame, violet is transformative power, and it is both breathtaking and majestic.

Silver is a very powerful cleanser and cleaner, and it is also a great strengthener. When you clean something up and clear something out, you are saying, "You cannot stay here!" Stronger boundaries are instantly created, and the whole system becomes reinforced. The surfaces of things also change, and everything is made shiny and new again. This is like scrubbing out the inside of a pot so that the silver can shine through.

Gold is another kingly color. At one time, the Earth had great veins of gold running through its crust. The perfection of gold instantly gave—and continues to give—everyone great pleasure. Everyone knows that gold is beyond special, and that it holds great value. While gold is often associated with wealth and money, another way to think about the gold standard is to know your own inner value, beyond the shadow of a doubt.

Pink is energy in blossom. Pink moves with the beat of a heart, and with a wisdom that knows more than anyone can even imagine. Pink combines great power and great delicacy. This color is extremely soft yet incredibly strong. Pink is the almost-nothing that can mean absolutely everything, like the tenderest gesture offered to a person in need, or the incomparable vibrancy of a blossoming rose. Pink can go into the darkest *and* into the brightest places and hold things that are too tender to be held, and then bring them forward, into the world. *Pink is a superpower.*

The color black is often associated with struggle—with facing a dark enemy. Black also calls to mind associations of power. It is not always the power of light. It can be dark power, like black magic. While the Man in Black can appear as a frightening source of conflict and opposition, you can also think of black as being a color of natural decomposition, like compost. Sometimes compost is called "black gold". From the struggle and the change come the richness, and there is new life.

There really is no color white. That is the irony, because white is all color with light. Just look at the sunlight shining on newly fallen snow. At first, you think it is only white. But if you look more closely, you see that it is every color—and that all of the colors are luminous, and they are all dancing together in the light. If black is the rich compost of the earth, then white is the air moving and shifting all around us. It is the play of snowflakes falling through the sky, falling through the light, and dancing in the wind.

P.S. You may also be interested in knowing that the companion guide opens with the image of teachers receiving an invitation to the Schools of Color, which I describe as an invitation to a really great party. As soon as the teachers and their students arrive, it feels like everyone is walking straight into a rainbow.

Is that creative, or what?

It's all just part of the magic...

Note Regarding Issues of Confidentiality

In compliance with the federal standards of the United States Health Insurance Portability and Accountability Act (HIPAA), within this volume particular details relating to specific individuals have been altered or generalized so as to omit any identifiable data. These precautions are consistent with HIPAA compliance while preserving issues of confidentiality, particularly as specified under "The Privacy Rule", The Belmont Report, and the Department of Health and Human Services Office for Human Research Protections, including The Common Rule and subparts B, C, and D of the Health and Human Service specifications as outlined in the Code of Federal Regulations (CFR) at 45 CFR 164 and 165, which specifies the "safe harbor" method of de-identification. By adopting this approach, the stories are presented in such a way as to make the subjects visible *and* to acknowledge the legal and ethical frameworks that make such representations possible at all. Thus, while the descriptions of encounters with patients and caregivers accurately reflect the nature of our interactions, and while the italicized texts are transcriptions of people's statements, these elements are generically worded, thus rendering the subjects anonymous.

This work has been favorably reviewed by two independent Institutional Review Boards (IRBs) at Rice University and at the M.D. Anderson Cancer Center.

About the Author and Illustrators

Marcia Brennan, Ph.D. is a career educator and an award-winning teacher and author. She is the Carolyn and Fred McManis Professor of Humanities at Rice University, where she also serves as Professor of Art History and Professor of Religious Studies. She is the author of ten monographs and exhibition catalogs. Her book *Painting Gender, Constructing Theory: The Alfred Stieglitz Circle and American Formalist Aesthetics* (MIT Press) was awarded the Georgia O'Keeffe Museum Research Center Book Prize. Among her numerous art historical volumes, she is the co-author of *Modern Mystic: The Art of Hyman Bloom* (Distributed Art Publishers), which was produced in conjunction with a major retrospective exhibition held at the Boston Museum of Fine Arts. She has also developed complementary research areas in literary aesthetics and psychosocial oncology. Since 2009, she has served as Artist In Residence in the Department of Palliative, Rehabilitation, and Integrative Medicine at the University of Texas M.D. Anderson Cancer Center. In 2021 she expanded this practice to serve as Literary Artist at the Hospital of the University of Pennsylvania, where she works in general oncology and transplantation oncology. Her creative clinical work has resulted in the publication of three volumes, the most recent of which is *A Rose From Two Gardens: Saint Thérèse of Lisieux and Images of the End of Life* (University of California Medical Humanities Press). She is the recipient of fellowships from the American Council of Learned Societies and the Samuel H. Kress Foundation. Throughout her career, she has been honored with 13 awards or recognitions for her teaching, including being selected four times as the recipient of Rice University's George R. Brown Award for Superior Teaching. In addition to teaching at Rice, she has also taught sessions at Baylor College of Medicine, and at the University of Texas McGovern Medical School. She lives in Houston, Texas.

Hannah Li studied Cell Biology & Genetics and Visual Arts at Rice University. Her enthusiasm for science and illustration has deeply influenced the way she views the world around her. She hopes to combine art with medicine, research, and storytelling in her future career as a physician-scientist.

Madison Zhao studies Neuroscience, Visual Arts, and Medical Humanities at Rice University. Her background in science and art informs her aspirations of becoming a physician who sees the value of both within a healthcare context. She is passionate about using art to uplift her community, and she works on projects ranging from book illustrations to hospital murals.

Description of *The Colors of Life*

Exploring Life Experience Through Color and Emotion

Marcia Brennan, Ph.D.

Illustrations by Hannah Li and Madison Zhao.

This book explores life experience through color and emotion.

What if I told you that you could explore the color blue for a thousand years? Red for a thousand years? Yellow for a thousand years? What if I told you that there were many different levels of learning, and that you could go through elementary school level, middle school level, high school level, or even college level in the different schools of color? Would you want to know more? If the answer is yes, then I have some wonderful news: You have just been invited to enter the Schools of Color!

This book adopts a unique prismatic approach to the study of color and emotion. The guiding concept of *The Colors of Life* is that it would be possible to study color and emotion for thousands of years and still never learn everything that these important subjects had to teach us. In addition to the seven primary spectral colors, the book examines pink, silver, gold, and black and white. Throughout the text, interwoven discussions of color and emotion are offered as concrete examples of character education, which lies at the very heart of Social and Emotional Learning (SEL). SEL is a pedagogical rubric that focuses on children's ability to integrate thinking, emotions, and behavior. The narratives, images, and exercises featured in this book engage SEL subjects through experiential learning activities, imaginative visualizations, reflective journaling exercises, creative writing prompts, and related visual arts projects. These activities provide a vibrant framework to explore powerful emotions such as confidence, anger, self-respect, vulnerability, strength, compassion, generosity, wonder, gratitude, humility, and many others.

Featuring more than 50 original color illustrations, the book engages a strong visual aesthetic so that core concepts are reinforced through complementary expressions of language and imagery. Through this approach, *The Colors of Life* promotes the accessibility of humanistic subjects among students who might not otherwise feel comfortable engaging with the Humanities, yet who will draw on these tools and insights throughout their education and well beyond.

Ultimately, the study of color and emotion holds real power to transform how people see the world, how they see others, and how they live their lives. This book teaches readers how to extend these themes into life and into meaning, and how to believe them soulfully.